Dear B,

Your energy + s
possible – thank you,
help along the way. I hope
the story makes you feel
inspired!!

BREAKFAST WITH
BAILS

What a Dying Coach
Taught Me About
Life, Learning & Leadership

Paddy Steinfort

XO

Allure Publishers
1 Allure Crt
Glen Waverley, VIC, 3150
Australia

Ordering Information:
Quantity sales. Special discounts are available on quantity purchases by corporations, associations, and others. For details, contact the publisher at the address above, or visit www.breakfastwithbails.com.

Printed in the United States of America

Publisher's Cataloging-in-Publication data
Steinfort, Paddy.
Breakfast With Bails: What a Dying Coach Taught Me About Life, Learning and Leadership / Paddy Steinfort.
ISBN 978-0-646-94856-0
1. Memoir. 2. Coaching. 3. Leadership. 4. Social psychology 5. Education & Development

First Published 2015

Praise From Authors

"A moving story about a great man. The wisdom from a dying coach's final days is reminiscent of Tuesdays with Morrie."
Adam Grant, *New York Times Bestselling Author,* **Give & Take** *and* **Originals**

"Breakfast With Bails is an inspiring story... The messages he leaves us with are surprising, simple truths that leaders in any arena - whether you are a coach, manager, mother, or teacher - can all live by. This book will not only change the way you lead – it will change the way you live your life. Buy it, read it, live it."
Jon Gordon, *bestselling author,* **The Energy Bus** *and* **Training Camp**

Praise From Coaches

"Bails really shone out from the pack. He could see people from a different point of view. His generous heart worked tirelessly to find the good in his players... he believed in them, he cared for them, gave them his time & knowledge. They succeeded. We succeeded."
Mark Williams, *2004 Premiership coach, Port Adelaide FC*

"The memories I have of Bails will stay with me forever. The biggest thing I learnt from him: he had empathy for all of his players. This book will give you an understanding of a truly great man."
Brad Green, *Assistant Coach, North Melbourne FC*

Praise From Players

"This book is a must read - Bails was a legend, a unique character with great humour, and he could always tell a good story. He really cared about us, and I'll always remember the things he taught me, both about football but even more as a person. Paddy Steinfort has done an amazing job!"
Taylor Walker, *Captain, Adelaide FC*

"Breakfast With Bails brought back so many amazing memories of this very humorous and extremely caring bloke. Im so glad his views on life and coaching will live on through this book."
Rory Sloane, *2013 Best & Fairest, Adelaide FC*

This book is dedicated
to Caron, the woman
who helped shape the man
who helped shape so many men

Contents

WARMUP

WARMUP

| | | |

The game of life hands the average person many teachers over time. Most pass by in a flash, forgotten almost before they are out of sight.

Some guides give us strong direction for a short while, but their guidelines become blurred without immediate contact.

Then there are those rare mentors that exert only a subtle force on us at first contact, but whose impact defies the laws of physics and time. Instead of fading, it grows.

And when they are gone, when there's no contact at all, the effect multiplies. It's as if their presence was the last tackler to navigate before the message finally hit paydirt in our minds and our hearts.

Their lessons and approach to life stretch beyond the classroom, the sports field, or the office. These teachers have a rare ability to enter their subject's mind. But not through force, or tricks designed to sneak in the back way, but by just knocking at the side door and casually asking to come in and help.

And it's almost as if, by the sheer nature of their ability to get in there with minimal force, they have the right to stay forever.

We all remember our own versions of this sage guide: the high school teacher who was different from the rest; the tutor at university who just got how tough the material was to understand; the office mentor who took the time to guide you through the politics, even though she had bigger things to do.

I've been lucky enough to have a couple of these teachers in my adult life. This book is about one of them. He was a football coach, and his name was Dean Bailey, but everybody just called him Bails.

Some of the toughest training sessions that Bails ever ran were his last, and to say they were a little different would be an understatement. The training stretched over a period of about three months – sometimes two sessions a week, sometimes none, depending on what the coach's health would allow – and more often than not involved a degree of discomfort. Questions were asked of all who attended, coach included. But those involved still fronted up right to the end.

Although there was no video to review, or numbers to rake over, there was one goal the sessions were constantly working toward: the compilation of this book, a no-frills game plan for learning and leadership from a football coach who can teach us a lot about life.

What's that I hear you say? Isn't there more to life than just football?

There sure is.

But there's also more to football than just football.

THE SETTING

His death sentence came late in 2013.

Up until then, he was always active, this "old" coach. Whether he was dragging himself through the water, swimming laps once the players were gone, or riding to and from our training base at West Lakes, come sunshine, rain or level 3 hurricane. On more than one occasion, each of the other coaches made some quip about the old guy they almost knocked off the road, bent over the handlebars, powering away with knees out like a schoolboy.

But after returning from a great off-season trip between the 2013 and 2014 seasons, something started slowing him down.

It was a simple cough at first: a bit chesty, and presumably a result of the combined fun he had during the break. He had attended a High Performance sports conference in London with the team's head coach, Brenton Sanderson - Sando to those close to him - and then followed that up with an extended holiday in Europe, one he and his wife Caron had thoroughly enjoyed. After a harrowing few of years involving power battles, a sacking, a league investigation and subsequent suspension for Dean, it was a welcome relief for the couple. Caron had been through almost as much as Dean, and they immersed themselves in the getaway.

The cough seemed a pretty open and shut case that didn't take a genius to work out: x number of weeks over y number of cities with an infinite number of red wines = lowered immune system. Add the constant air conditioning on the flights, and it was obvious this was just a cold that would be kicked as soon as we were back at base and into the healthy routine again.

And with the plans he and Sando had hatched for pushing the boundaries of the training environment this pre-season, Bails would be more active than ever. The time the two coaches spent together at the conference was invaluable, allowing them to formulate a plot that would take the team back to the top end of the table, where they both thought the talent level belonged.

They had talked strategy and handling of certain players, then designed new drills and rituals that would increase pressure on players and prepare them mentally for when games were on the line. Most of these strategies were based on competition with consequences, but the two competitive beasts were particularly pleased with the idea of a Players vs. Coaches challenge, where the coaching group would compete with selected players, with a penalty riding on the outcome.

The enthusiasm was obvious in emails to the other coaches still on holidays, and as soon as the pesky little cough was gone, Bails would be all in.

But this pesky little cough wasn't that easy to shake.

Cough syrup didn't do it at first, so he took more. He carried a bottle with him to work after the first week back, mostly because it seemed to keep it at bay long enough to allow him to talk about what he loved - football - without a cough interrupting his flow. When he was in the zone, Bails could talk for hours about the game or a certain player's strengths or weaknesses.

Like a player coming up through the ranks, the cough was graduating levels as the weeks progressed. It was moving up from "pesky" to "annoying" now.

The bike riding was the first thing to go, simply because the crisp morning air left him even more cough-ridden for the rest of the day. There weren't many players around just yet, so he hoped that taking it easy for a week would allow him to get on top of it, primed for when full training resumed.

But it didn't.

A week or so after the players were back in full training, the new tradition of Coaches vs. Players challenge was a hit, and both groups had been equally cocky and nervous heading into a goal kicking challenge. Players A, B, C and D were matched against coaches W, X, Y and Z, and on the line was a "Malcolm": a relatively innocent 20m shuttle run that would be a cinch for any suburban athlete, but for the fact that every ten metres you were forced to drop to touch your chest on the ground and push back up to keep running. If the selected competitors lost, the whole group was doomed to feel the burn.

As the final kick for the coaches sailed wide, the players celebrated with enthusiasm and bravado, trash talking the dejected coaching group before they had even lined up for the first minute. As a penalized member myself, this was my first Malcolm, and pretty soon I was aware of nothing more than my thumping heart rate, shrunken airways and burning chest.

Even the ache in my legs faded into the background as I willed my way to the end; it would be a cardinal sin, a failure as a man for a coach to not get through this. You couldn't stop, unless you were comfortable with the ribbing you would get for the next twelve months.

By the time the torture was over, I could barely think beyond the burn in my throat, the thumping in my chest, and the voice in my head: a mix of curse words and questions. How the hell had I gotten so out of shape?

I knew the answer: like many coaches and managers in pro sports, I had spent my "holiday" buried in the search for The Secret: the magic pill that would separate us from the pack. We were chasing the ultimate goal, sporting immortality, and it was our job to build plans that would make those dreams come true.

It wasn't until we came off the track, still breathless, that someone told me about Bails.

He had stopped midway, claiming he couldn't actually breathe, and headed into his office. There he sat, gasping for air and not having much success.

He saw the club doctor, who pressed a stethoscope around various points on his chest and in quick order suggested he get to a hospital to see a specialist. Within hours, an x-ray had revealed fluid on his left lung, and he was diagnosed with pneumonia.

Not one to feel sorry for himself or to take things too seriously, he shot a quick note from his hospital bed to Sando, who relayed the message to us:

Guys,

Bails spent last night in Flinders & had 1.5 litres of fluid drained from his lungs.

In his words, a 'combo of Peroni, gelato & Italian red wine'....so at least they didn't drain any of his sense of humour out.

No set time for a return date, just plenty of rest, but he will be home from the hospital this afternoon.
In the meantime, Steinfort & Nutta will pick up his work from a coaching point of view, but we all might need to chip in to cover his guys.

I don't think the whole world needs to know, so we'll keep it in the house for the time being.

Thanks
Sando

Typical manly communication from the patient, and from within the football department. The message was clear: we would power on, some of us would step up to cover him and we would be even stronger when he came back.

But despite the excess drainage, the condition was no better a day or two later, and Bails remained in the hospital.

When further tests were ordered, brows became furrowed and conversations about how Bails was doing became shorter and more awkward. Those who had asked more than once understood it wasn't progressing as it should.

THE OPPONENT

Finally, on a hot, dry day in December, Dean and Caron were handed the news: Bails had an aggressive cancer in his lungs. They didn't know what type of cancer, as the source hadn't yet been identified.

Which meant they couldn't give a definite answer on whether it could be beaten or not.

"How did I get it?" Dean asked.

Nobody could answer him. Those who believed in the links between stress and cancer bit their tongue – now was not the time for finger-pointing. A fight was on the cards first, and more info was needed.

"Is it spreading?"

"We can't be sure right now," came the clinical reply. "Further tests are required."

"Am I going to die?"

"Until we know more," the doctor replied in a practiced, measured voice, "we can't give you any specific answers. But we can say this condition is life limiting."

More words followed, but to both Bails and Caron, they were simply white noise, like the ambient murmur of a crowd behind the voice of a commentator. What they heard crystal clear was the most delicately worded sledgehammer:

This condition is life limiting.

So while the disease Bails now knew was cancer continued to grow inside him, the former working-class footballer was consigned to a relatively ambiguous treatment regime until further details came to light. For a man known for his clinical dissection of every detail in both his and the opposition's game plan, this vague opponent unnerved him, though he wouldn't let that on to many. It would be a challenge he would tackle in the same way he did his backyard games as a kid: not knowing where it might end up, just trying to get better, one challenge at a time.

When word reached the coaches, the reaction was stunned silence. Then the inevitable questions came, mirroring those that Bails and Caron had asked their doctor and which would be repeated by the players when they were told: how bad is it? When did it start? Is it terminal? How long will he be off? Can we visit him?

Then, in more hushed tones or away from the main group, the more personal questions came, reflections of those with families putting themselves in his shoes: how is Caron? And the boys? Do they think their dad is going to die? What will they do if he does?

Vague answers gave rise to a sense of hope that this would be a similar story to that of our Head of Physical Performance Team, Nick Poulos, who had fought cancer and won almost a decade ago now. Or, at worst, that it would be a courageous battle similar to that of the legendary Jim Stynes, stretching over multiple years and allowing us to prepare for the loss of a close friend.

But it belied the serious, vicious nature of Bails' affliction, which was attacking his lung with all the aggression of a tackle from the best defender in the league.

A defender that was on top, and not likely to ease up.

THE COACH

Before I worked with him, my perception of the coach Dean Bailey was probably similar to that of anyone else who hadn't yet met him in person, based purely on snippets fed to the public via cutaways to the coaches' box during games, in post-match press conferences, or in the all too rare article that actually provided more than a glib quote or media friendly cliché.

In these short glimpses, tainted often by the stress of another Demons loss, or the growing pressure around his job security later in his senior coaching experience, he seemed like part exasperated teacher, part unflustered poker player.

Rarely over the top in his reactions, his calm, methodical approach - despite constant setbacks - suggested he was either trying to bluff his way through to the next hand without losing what little support he had left in his stack, or that he knew something the public didn't. Something about the students he had, the game they were learning, or how good their teacher was.

In late 2011, I learned that it was a little bit of all of the above.

On a typically still October evening in Adelaide - a little chillier than normal for the South Australian capital given it was the day before November began - I had stepped off the last Virgin flight for the night, not quite sure what to expect as I arrived in a new town.

I'd received instructions by email while I was in the U.S. from Maria Ballestrin, the football secretary (i.e., the person who makes things happen) at the Adelaide Crows, where I was about to start the very next day:

Hi Paddy,

Just to keep in touch, I hope you are having a great time.

When you arrive on Sunday 30 October, Dean Bailey will be picking you up.

Dean has found and is renting a three-bedroom place in Brighton. His family won't be moving immediately, and he has volunteered to have you stay with him until you find your own place.

I know you are on holiday, but I am sure you don't mind me touching base.

Regards,
Maria.

Grabbing my phone from my pocket, I shot a text to the other new coach I'd be staying with while I found my feet in Adelaide. The reply came back swiftly.

'Round the corner. See you out front in 5.

No fuss, no extra details – simple, direct.

By the time I was at the back of the car, bag in hand, Bails was already there with one hand reaching for the bag, extending the other to welcome me.

He was a shortish guy, unassuming almost, except when he walked – chest out, feet slightly splayed, arms anchored steadily by his side even when walking quickly. The combined effect of these three idiosyncrasies was the impression of a regular guy, calm and contained, but still ready for anything the game of life might want to throw at him.

Contradicting this puffed-out, chest-first entry to the room was a handshake that was almost ambivalent – relaxed grip, no attempt to display more emotion than was necessary, average contact time. Not overdoing it to create false engagement, but not underselling the person either. Pretty much in the middle.

"How was the flight?" Bails asked after the standard exchange of "Gday mate, great to meet you."

"Yeah, not bad," was my reply, almost as standard as the greeting. "Got the double of exit row and seat next to me was empty. Poor man's business class!"

Bails chuckled, and we were off to a good start. The rest of the ride back to Bails' place was more like a cruise than an airport transfer. Or perhaps more like a chilled out wine and coffee tour.

"Just bear with me here," Bails mumbled through the parking ticket held between his teeth as he fumbled for his wallet in the console.

"No dramas."

A short pause while he negotiated the exit at the airport.

"So do you like coffee?" Bails started up again as the car left the airport.

"I can't live without it," I told him, only half-joking.

"Good. I think we'll get along then. How do you have it?"

"Short. Black. Get the caffeine straight to the veins." I had slapped the inside of my elbow, a visual gag that Bails appreciated with a singular "Ha!" and a wry smile.

"I'll tell you how I have mine tomorrow when you're going to get them," he quipped. "There's this great place around the corner from our place that we will become very familiar with, I think."

He had said "our place." Was the rest of the Bailey clan waiting back there for me? My thoughts would've normally run away with me, but the casual energy of Bails and his conversational skills dragged me from my mind and back to the present.

This ability to command attention without craving it was something I'd become familiar with over the next few weeks as we shared breakfasts, drives, dinners, and plenty of coffees in between. But here in this first face-to-face encounter was a glimpse into the coach who wasn't shown on the TV, or in the carefully scripted press conferences.

Our first encounter the night before and at breakfast that first morning was a perfect case in point: with nothing to go on but a shared drive home and some banter over breakfast, I would still have been able to pick the adjectives those closest to him would eventually use to eulogize the man they knew better than any: humble, humourous, headstrong, and human.

In the glow of what was possible for our new team, we both had no idea what lay ahead. Sometimes you don't know the value of a certain time until it's gone.

In those whirlwind days at a new team, I lived with him for a few weeks, sharing breakfast, coffee breaks, and dinners. We talked sport, politics, single life, married life, football life, bachelor life, favourite foods, favourite TV shows, favourite books. I enjoyed tales from his six years in the game as a player at a powerhouse Essendon team, but even more entertaining were his coaching stories. I heard how he was hired by the legendary Kevin Sheedy as an untried development coach at his old team. I learned of his premiership triumph at Port Adelaide. And I discovered the dark side of the game as he recounted his struggles, and eventual sacking, as head coach at Melbourne.

We got to know each other in the way football staff often did – intimately, intensely, but at the same time with professional boundaries that kept us from going too deeply into each others' business.

And then I moved out.

Partly because I wanted to be my own man; mostly because I didn't want to get too close. I was keen to build my own life, live like a single bachelor, and were it not for us sharing the same workplace and forty-five players to develop, I would probably have lost touch.

This hit and run approach to new friendships was a habit of mine that started when my playing career ended. I had begun my career as a professional footballer at the age of 18, coming straight out of high school with stars in my eyes and dreams in my head. I was a first-round draft pick, destined for big things. In those years, I was a total team player, a huge giver.

I'd left the game five years later with a regrettable record to my name: the player who spent the longest time with a single team without ever playing a game. Injuries were not kind to me, and on the rare occasion I was fit, other players who I had happily helped as a good teammate had gone past me.

When I was cut, that word was as apt as any to describe the feeling I had at having so many "friendships" severed all at once: cut to the bone. As I struggled on my own with those emotions, I concluded that the world would turn on you despite your best efforts, regardless of how loyal or social you might be.

I'd learned what I thought were the most important lessons of my adult life: Look after yourself, and take whatever chances you can to get ahead. From that point on my purpose in life was to stand out. With this relentless chase for the next edge, the next promotion, the next upgrade, I was unwittingly becoming a rare commodity in the industry I loved but had run away from – a former player, with scientific qualifications, experience in international sports, and as close to 10,000 hours of leadership training as one could find in a 30-year-old.

This played out for a decade in my personal life too – relationships came and went, as did jobs. Always looking out for myself first. Always striving to step up to the next level. That's how I came to find myself working in Adelaide with Bails. And that's how I came to move out of his house after only a month or so. I had to stand on my own and handle my own business.

That's what winners do, right?

THE PLAN

I had my business face on when I entered the hospital room for the first time on my own. But Bails had no inkling of formality or awkwardness about him, even though I had already set the scene for a more in-depth conversation with a semi-formal text message.

> Bails, u up for a visitor Sat or Sunday morning?
> Got an idea I wanna' run past you...

The reply was typically short and sharp.

> Either sat or sun doesn't matter

And in keeping with the business-like setup, I replied in double time to lock the appointment.

What I hadn't expected was to see his sons when I walked in. It was so normal, yet unnerving: Bails was kicking back in bed, looking as healthy as he had at his desk only days earlier. His two sons, Mitchell and Darcy, sat at the foot of his bed in standard hospital visitors chairs.

Darcy, the younger of the two at 19, was in great shape thanks to being midway through a pre-season with the Glenelg Tigers himself. With a fresh haircut, his strawberry-blonde hair cropped short and swept to the side, he looked like a well-trained soldier.

Mitch's red hair was much more stark, thanks in part to it blending into a growing beard of the same colour. At 22 he was already a stocky young man with a barrel chest, almost an extreme caricature of what I imagine Bails would've been at that age. I first met Mitch when I lived with Bails, and his dry humour was as evident in person as Darcy's was through the text banter he would engage in with his dad on a nightly basis.

This scene was anything but humourous though. It had slapped me in the face as I entered his room. In any other context seeing a father and his two sons, who were now young men, sitting and chewing the fat would be heartwarming. But knowing the reason each of the actors was in this scene added an edge that was too sharp to swallow. Sitting with his sons would only make the emotions of the current struggle more intense. I could only imagine that at this point, Bails just wanted some normality from his friends. Talk about football, training, the weather. Hell, talk about anything other than what he was feeling. To ask questions about his emotions and what is important in life was to press on bones that were freshly broken, and would only confirm the break rather than fix it.

The dry Bailey humor was a dominant gene though, and all three of them possessed it in spades. They kept the conversation light for as long as the standard "summer-weather-football" banter lasted. After five minutes or so, putting his great sense for the feel of a room to use, Bails picked up that my idea may not have been the best for the boys. With the deft touch of a world-class communicator, he mentioned something about the boys going to get something to eat. Both left with a dry joke – like father, like son – and headed out into the corridor.

As I settled into the leather chair next to his bed, and the small talk about sport, training, and the weather was done, my business face wasn't so strong anymore. But my ear for a lull in conversation was still sharp, and when the opportunity came up, I took a deep breath and jumped in.

"Can I ask you something?"

"You just did," Bails replied, dry as ever.

I couldn't help but chuckle at the fact that he'd still make bad jokes a week into his first hospitalization.

"You got me." I paused, still unsure if this was a good idea. "Have you ever read the book *Tuesday's With Morrie*?" I threw it up in the air like an alley-oop, with a mix of hesitation and guilt, spiked with a shot of hope.

"Yeah, I have, yeah – great book." He stopped fiddling with the bed controls and looked up at me with an eyebrow cocked. "Why's that?"

All of a sudden, the words I had practiced in the car were gone, vanished like the training of an expert golfer who has a case of the yips. I had described the idea to plenty of people, and everyone loved it. Even more importantly, everyone I had canvassed was pretty sure Bails would be okay with it too.

But I didn't want him to feel like he was being used, especially at a time like this. He had more than his fair share of guys in white coats prodding and probing him, talking about him as if he weren't in the room and asking him questions that he had to answer honestly, but couldn't know what his answers might be adding up to.

The last thing he needed right now was another person treating him like a science experiment, assessing what he said and collating responses and probing deeper and ignoring his emotions, his humanity. I had little knowledge of cancer, but a fairly intimate knowledge of the powerlessness that comes with the hospital gown. Eight operations in as many years during a career wrecked by injuries allowed me that insight at least.

I almost pulled out, playing with the idea of making up an excuse for bringing it up. But then a memory of our last breakfast reminded me why I couldn't.

Swedish Tarts café in Henley Beach is a chic little hole in the wall that barely had room for us when we showed up on a sunny spring day, so we took the only table that was available. Sitting down among the cool kids and assorted soccer mums, I thought the conversation we had planned to have - about how we wanted to raise the bar for the team this pre-season and which players we needed to target most - would be stilted a little, especially given we were clad head to toe in Crows training apparel.

"Sometimes you get to set a course when the waters are calm." He sipped his tea and coughed loudly, drawing the ire of a young couple on a coffee date at the table next to us. "When you are first in charge, or in a new position, the waters are calm. Hell, most of the time in those cases the waters are even flowing in the direction you want, and it's smooth sailing – the winds are gentle, the bloody dolphins are even swimming next to you, the sun is shining... anyone can set the course in those conditions."

The sensitive approach might have been the way to go had the coffee been with another coach. But Bails wasn't one for beating around the bush.

"I had to deal with a lot of wankers back at Melbourne," he said loudly enough to startle at least one eavesdropper. "Know-it-alls who questioned something that they initially supported, just 'cos other people started asking questions. The plan hadn't changed. The expectations hadn't changed. Only thing that had changed was people's opinions."

"Problem is, the waters never stay calm – there'll be things that come up that will make people question the plans and the program you set, and it'll even make you question it yourself. And you should do that occasionally, but the better coaches and leaders are able to stick to it – to press into the rough weather and say 'screw it – I set that plan with this end in mind, and I know it's right.'"

"When you've put something in motion that you believe in, you've gotta see it through."

And so, like Bails taught me to, I pressed on.

I told him about the idea to catch up with him regularly to talk in depth about life. I stumbled over the fact that I didn't want it to be about death. I clumsily mentioned that I wanted to focus on football, mostly the good stuff, but occasionally we might touch on some bad times too. I threw in that I wanted to use some of it with the players while he was away from the team. Then I quickly moved on to the fact that I would be flexible and work around him, mostly so we didn't hover too long on the fact he might not be back for a while.

All the while, I avoided eye contact, almost ashamed that I was asking a guy who was fighting the biggest battle of his life if he could do a favour for myself and the guys he was teaching. I tried to lighten the mood with a little joke at the end about Wikileaks. I don't know if it worked, but he spoke up, maybe to put me out of my misery.

"Yeah," he said off-hand, with a slight wheeze. "Yeah, that's fine. Not sure if anything that comes out could be considered wisdom, but that should be okay."

I closed my eyes and did a mental fist-pump, thrilled that I was ballsy enough to actually ask the question in the first place.

"But they'll have to be short, 'cos the treatment is taking it out of me at the moment," he added. "I'm already losing my hair." Bails had been bald for years. Good to see his sense of humor was still intact.

I laughed. "Of course mate," I agreed, "I was only thinking twenty or thirty minutes at a time." We then went over the basic details: how I would send him some questions in advance, so he wouldn't get caught on the hop; how I would use the Dictaphone on my phone to record the chats; which times would suit; how I would bring some brain food and coffee to make sure we were both sharp; and, what we would refer to the project as: *Breakfast with Bails*.

"Sounds good," I concluded. A full stop on a full-on request.

A stillness filled the room, perhaps accentuated for me by the lowering of my anxious heart rate and the quiet of the TV between points in the Australian Open tennis.

"You want some more chocolate?" I asked.

"Does Dolly Parton sleep on her back?"

Back to normal for now. Sports. Sugar. Sarcasm. The complicated stuff can wait until the next visit.

SCRIMMAGE ONE

ATTACK

ATTACK

| | | | |

"Dead Man Coaching" was the headline that had stuck in Bails'
mind.

And it was the first thing that ran along his mental ticker as he ran
into the author shortly afterwards, and the air turned icy in the media
room at the MCG that day mid-way through the 2011 season.

Bails would normally talk in a collegial manner with the media folk
he respected. He would sidle up to the legendary Mike Sheahan and ask,
without a hint of inflection or malice, if he had any new rumours for
him. He'd talk straight and true with the best investigative journalist
in the industry, Caroline Wilson, known for a forthright style herself.
He was known to joke - deadpan, as always - at the beginning of, and
sometimes during, press conferences, and warmed to those who got his
subtle jokes.

On this winter day, however, he was anything but warm with
Mark Robinson - known to industry insiders and public alike simply as
"Robbo." After what had felt like a long, deliberate and at times
personal campaign by Robbo to throw him to the wolves before allowing
the results to speak, Bails wasn't in the mood for small talk.

The temperature variance between the two of them had begun as a
simmering heat in pre-season before a ball had even bounced, when
Robbo arbitrarily placed him at "High" on his coach's pressure index.
This was despite the slow and steady improvement to that point of a
young Demons squad in each of his three years at the helm, and the fact

that in the year just passed the team had doubled their number of wins, and their percentage, from the previous year.

It grew to a roaring fire in week 6. With a 2-2-1 record that was on track to better the previous years mark easily - the two losses being to teams that would both make the final 4 that year and a draw with the team that would win the 2012 premiership - the 'Dead Man Coaching' article seemed devoted solely to turning up the heat on Bails. Listing eight separate reasons that Bails should be sacked, with varying degrees of truth to them and a lot of "ifs" to connect the threads, Robbo put the Melbourne coach's role on center stage for all of the other media programs to debate. He had knowingly ignited a debate that would continue for months despite an improving record and some big wins.

In their professional roles, the two weren't that different. Neither was known for their airs and graces, bringing a "what you see is what you get" attitude. Not often one to apologise for his words, Robbo offered an olive branch in the form of an admission at first.

"Mate," he began, and Bails looked at him dispassionately, "Jimmy's given me a clip, he's given me a real clip on radio."

Bails' lack of response was unnerving, and so Robbo continued.

"Yeah, I went too far; the heading was no good. But you gotta' understand I don't write the headings."

Bails held in a chuckle, knowing full well that the offending words were written in the article too. The instincts of the young footballer inside wanted to rear up and attack the provocation - to strike out with words in the same way he might've taken a fist to solve an issue with an opponent in his playing days. Three different words replaced the headline in Bails' head now: "Bullshit, Robbo. Weak."

"Yeah no worries," Bails ignored his emotions and responded calmly. His delivery was as dry as ever, leaving Robbo wondering if he really did accept the apology. "That's okay."

Bails turned to get on with his duties and left Robbo to his. No need to make a scene that could be more fodder for the fire. There were plenty of "supporters" online who would help with that.

One thing Robbo's article had done for Bails was make him acutely aware of the existence of a Facebook group set up for the purpose of calling for the sacking of their coach. The online petition was posted the night of the Demons' 54-point loss in just their fifth game of the season, on an away trip to the Eagles, a powerful team who would go on to finish the season in fourth place.

By the next morning, in just twelve hours, the group had already gained seventy-five members. With the help of Robbo's inflammatory article, the electronic emotions of supporters would spread to other forums over the course of that weekend and the following weeks. All educated commentators, of course, and no irrational reactions.

"..Bailey deserves nothing, hes strike rate is deplorable, i cant fathom how fans still defend the loser.."

*"..gold plated ****ing clown named Dean Bailey.."*

*"..I will not be taking out a MFC membership whilst this ****head is living in Melbourne let alone coaching them.."*

*"..Yep, **** off Bailey. This is vomit.."*

*"..if i performed at work the way that **** wit bailey does i would be standing in the centrelink line, the sooner that losers gone the better, what a dead set non winning ****ing loser he is…*

*"…****ing embarresing, i wish that loser would just quit.."*

*"..im not going back to the footy until that ****ing loser is sacked.."*

Without checking the internet, Bails knew that it was full of angry messages, mostly aimed at the coach. This wasn't unfamiliar territory - verbal abuse was part and parcel of the show. He was well aware from his time as a player, and even more so as an assistant coach, that the head coach held the hottest seat in the game. "Lucky I have thick skin, *and the world's hairiest back," he would joke. But the personal nature of some of the barbs – both online and in the papers - was starting to wear thin.*

What irked Bails most wasn't so much the faceless nature of the attacks online, or the professionals who would never have to account for the injuries their words may inflict. It was the fact the players he loved were bombarded on Twitter - a service Bails had never really wrapped his head around - where the faceless abuse was flowing freely. The uneducated trolls were out in full force.

For now, he just had to ignore the people yelling at him - figuratively and literally - while he read the latest figures for the business he was leading. Forget what the taxi driver or the talkback caller says about your manhood. Don't take any notice of the man with the megaphone, calling for your head.

Go home to your family, and concentrate on providing for them while you can.

TRAINING

BLOCK ONE

TOUCH
WE TALK ABOUT PEOPLE & PAIN

From a distance, the absolute stillness of the summer Saturday and the lack of any other humans would have made the cars in the hospital parking lot appear as lizards, basking in the hot sun as the day built to its fiery crescendo.

Up close, though, I saw only asphalt and shimmering metal. As I walked from my car to the entrance, squinting hard to keep out the glare, I was barely aware of the oppressive heat thanks to the list of lingering questions about Bails that I was wrestling with in my mind.

With our first session flagged for this week, I had ticked multiple boxes to shape just how what I saw as the most crucial chat would unfold. Making sure Bails was okay with it was obviously the biggest step. Sorting out what I might ask was another one, and I had addressed that in the car almost as soon as I left the hospital after my last visit, using my phone to jot notes that were rushing into my mind like a home crowd invading the field after a landmark victory.

Prepping for hard conversations was something I was used to, given that the majority of my professional life since being a footballer involved extracting information from others, often in trying circumstances or under the emotional duress that an injury, setback or personal problem brings along with it.

Career-threatening injury? No sweat – I'd had more than my share personally and dealt with plenty of other athletes in that position. Embarrassing feedback from your peers? I could handle someone in that seat even if I were hogtied and blindfolded.

Problems at home with mum / dad / wife / girlfriend / housemate / dog / cat? Give me your best curveball, and I'll still hit it out of the park.

This, however, was one conversation for which I hadn't had any preparation. So much remained unanswered thanks to a lack of past experiences, or mental game tape as I referred to it with some players, anything that would give me some sense of where things might go.

Now that he knows there's an agenda to the visits, will he act differently?

Can I say 'I understand' when I really have no idea?

Is it ok to say the big 'C' word?

Will he take back his permission if it becomes too emotional?

Despite my best mental acrobatics and prediction abilities, I was unable to answer any of those. So in an attempt to keep things light at the start, the setup for the first session had been deliberately offhand about the first round of chemo he had received the day before, and more focused on issues of time and taste:

> Bails, hope today went ok. Was thinking about coming in to visit sometime during the day tomorrow.. Is there anytime you'd prefer visitors?

Visitor traffic was obviously light in the hospital that evening because his reply had come back minutes later.

> Mate, mid morning is fine

> Sweet, will c'ya then

And then, almost as an afterthought.

> How does chocolate treat you at the
> moment?

His reply was even quicker this time.

> Dark chocolate must be minimum 80%
> I prefer the dark chocolate and orange.

He also had an afterthought, perhaps more calculated than mine.

> I have a little fridge in my room.

I laughed out loud at this one – a regular occurrence when having text conversations with Bails.

> Roger that. Will see what I can
> rustle up.

Rarely one for effusive punctuation in his written communications, let alone his verbal ones, his response hinted at a genuine excitement that made perfect sense given his well known appreciation for gastronomic treats.

> Sweet !!!!

Thankfully, his enthusiasm was at the same level on my arrival. I could craft the story and say it was because he was looking so forward to sharing his insights. I could bend the truth even more and claim it was because my presence lit a spark in him that reminded him of when he was my age. In reality, it was the cargo I'd smuggled past the nurses that had him almost out of his bed. I had revealed it before we could engage in our standard casual handshake, admitting I didn't know which of the

500gm blocks to bring along with the orange and dark chocolate he mentioned – so I had just packed four.

"A couple of them are only 70 percent and 75 percent respectively," I confessed with a wry smile, "so if you can't get through them I'll put my hand up to help."

"Ha!" he let out a loud, lengthy chuckle, filling the stale room with life and startling a passing nurse.

"Ohhh-ho-ho Paddy," he buzzed as he reached out to examine the delivery. "You've outdone yourself here."

It was refreshing to see him in his normal modus operandi – the big kid trapped in an older man's body, still as filled with joy by sweet treats as an adolescent schoolboy.

This helped ease my stress about how this visit might go. While Bails negotiated the various wrappers that stood between him and his cacao fix, I took my iPhone out of my pocket, loaded the Dictaphone app and started recording the first session.

"Depends on what sort of sleep I've had the night before." With only the slightest of wheezes perceptible, Bails answers my first question about how he's feeling.

"Last night I didn't get to sleep till 4 o'clock you know. I'm that tired, but I pushed myself to get through to the end of the tennis. It's four all and 40 love, with Rafael, and I throw a couple of sleeping pills in, thinking they'll just..."

He makes a "cluck" sound with his tongue for effect here, and simultaneously shuts his eyelids and drops his head back, pausing for effect. For a moment, I think the patient in bed before me may have nodded off until he starts his dry narration again.

"...kick in, so I turn the lights off. And then I'm just floating, like 'I'm asleep here'. And then as soon as I've fallen asleep, I'm awake."

The disappointment and frustration are clear, his hand exasperatingly slapping the bed linen the same way he has slapped the desk of his coach's box for years.

"I dunno if I've had four or five hours or what. So I look at my phone, and it's 12 o'clock. I'd only fallen asleep an hour."

I consider how mixed up my mind is when I'm sleep deprived, and wonder what it must be like to have that feeling with a whopping side of "end-of-the-road worries" added on.

"I should be able to sleep right through, 'cos I am pretty drained. But generally the night before, if I've slept okay, normally my best time is in the morning."

Trying to lighten the mood, I change the subject to one he loves: people.

"Have many of the boys come in?"

"Most of the coaches have been in," he exhales, "and a few players & a couple of staff too." He begins thumbing through his mental rolodex, one that's seemingly arranged by nicknames: Sando, Tater, Jonah, Campo and Bicks, Truck, Tex and Sloaney, Triggy and Chappy, Kedge and the Rat, Pottsy, Dasher (and his wife), Lewy and Thomo. "I'm trying to think of who that other player is... man, I can see them sitting here, Lewy and Thomo, and..."

His voice trails off again as he stares blankly at the floor, searching for another player's name. Given how many guys he had coached over the years – more than a decade at the top level now, as well as a handful at lower levels – it could make for a long search.

For a moment he seemed lost amongst all the nicknames, surnames & numbers that are the default means of identification within any sports team. And then, with a burst of life and energy that was almost out of place for both the topic of conversation and the place it was being held, his eyebrows jumped as he blurted out the nickname of that final player.

"Sauce!"

"The big fella!" I respond in kind, swept up in the enthusiasm that had overcome him simply from remembering a name. This wasn't unusual for Bails. He could match the mood

31

of anyone at any given time, but also could bring you to his level without you even noticing.

"Big Saucey Jacobs," he settled back into his sitting position in the hospital bed, remembering where he was and the sombre mood that was part of the dress code in the oncology ward of a hospital. "Yeah, I got a text or two from some of the other boys too."

He almost sighed as he remembered his current isolation.

"Some of them aren't sure when they can come in," he continued, "or if they can come in at all. Other people just can't do it, you know? They can't face what's happening. I can hear 'em going, 'Oh I dunno about that... do I wanna go to the hospital?'"

We talk for a short while about the different characters in the team. To fans and media, the names we talk of are a collection of heroes, but to us they're just workmates and friends. The normality of the relationships inside the walls of the club was something common to all professional sports environments – insulation against the sometimes cruel world of critics and fickle fans – and it was a comfort to get back there when times were tough.

A silence falls over the room, or at least what would pass for silence in a hospital room in the middle of summer. The metronome of tennis shots playing steadily on TV, punctuated by the occasional conversation about holidays from the hallway, as the hospitals' employees went about their jobs. A normal Friday in January, aside from the fact I was sitting with a dying man.

This was now his normal though, or at least the world he occupied temporarily – not healthy enough for friends to visit as they normally would, but also not close enough to death's door to have them want to come and see him one more time. A cruel purgatory for Bails, who everyone knew was a people person at his core. It was a far cry from some of my earliest memories of this people person.

"Did I tell you we got a couple of psychology masters students as cadets?" I ask, changing tack from some serious stuff. In my mind it was a wise move to steer the conversation more towards Bails' interest in psychology. I was counting on his enthusiasm for the topic given that he wished he had done more of it earlier in his coaching career. "They're gonna come in and help us with the goal kicking data, zones for each player, each session."

I thought he might bite and take the conversation to coaching theory, or to a book he loved. Instead, more pressing, personal matters were front of mind.

"You know, young Mitchell Bailey is a sports science graduate, he's just finished."

"Is he?" I rolled with it.

"Yep. Graduates in March I think."

With full awareness of the end result Bails was aiming at for his son, I didn't hesitate to take the bait.

"Would he want to do some work? The cadets only get a little bit for the year."

"It depends," the father was now in the room. Coach Bailey had checked out for a second. "He's working at Glenelg, under 18s. But if it fits in, and all you've gotta do is record data..."

"He'd only have to be there for two sessions a week," I assured him.

"And it's gonna be training during the day?"

"Yep. I'll get his number off 'ya."

"In fact, Ill give it to 'ya right now," Bails wasn't going to waste time; cancer does that to you. "Gimme that phone over there, will 'ya?"

"That's mine," I referred to the one he pointed at. "This one's yours."

"If it fits in with him, that'd be ideal," he seemed more awkward teen now than authoritative father, "'cos, ahhh…"

His voice trailed off. A small quiver in his chin and the prolonged breath was the only giveaway that this was the first emotional hurdle we would face in our chats.

"I was gonna talk to Nick but may as well talk to you and Darren Burgess as well, and ask a favor to get my son into either Crows or Port. It's the next level for Mitch. He just needs a foot in the door; that's it. Even if it's stuff like this – if it's an hour here, an hour there, it might lead to something more steady down the track."

It was like the entire room, the entire hospital, had gone silent and was hanging on a dying father's every word right now. Even the curtains on the windows, waving with the air-conditioning only moments earlier, were now motionless.

"I know how the system works – if you get in there long enough, show you're enthusiastic and show your personality, you move into a job. Jobs in AFL aren't going backwards, particularly at ground level, there's gonna be a few more, so... If anything comes up, I'm sort of asking a big favor from you 'cos..."

He pauses as a young, attractive nurse knocks and sticks her head in the door.

"Excuse me, sorry," she apologised, "do you want me to make your bed now or later?"

"Ah, a little bit later if you could." Bails looked at me sideways, with a mischievous grin.

"No worries," the nurse replied, her people skills alerting her to the fact her timing may not have been ideal. She closes the door and leaves us to it.

"Dunno how," Bails raises his eyebrows with an incredulous look, "but she just got assigned to my room."

We both laugh. I try to grab on to the light relief that the joke had brought to the room, and share a funny story involving one of my many surgeries as a player. The story doesn't even register with Bails – his mind is still back on his son.

"So if you could help me out Paddy, with Mitch, that's all."

"Of course." Given how much Bails gave to others, including me, it was the least I could do. "If he's happy to help out with one or two sessions, I'd put him ahead of the other blokes for sure."

"That'd be good."

"Um..." Given the depth of the discussion to this point, I pause to contemplate whether it's time to dive in a bit deeper while the water is warm. Without too much thought, I decide it is.

I had been worried when I initially broached the idea for the sessions that Bails wouldn't want to talk about real personal stuff, so I started with what I intended to be a work related question:

"So what are you missing the most, mate? Not having been down for a while. What do you lie here and wish you were doing?"

The sensitivity of what I've just asked a man battling a terminal disease strikes me, and I attempt to lighten the request with a gag.

"Probly not work?"

I needn't have worried about the seriousness of my question. Bails' dry wit was there to release the pressure.

"Having sex with my wife, that's one thing."

The raw response startled me. "Okay, that's fair enough," I chuckled, glad for a moment that he had made a joke.

Only when I looked up to share our smiles, my sense of normality and the sense of the sacred caved in to form one big lump in my throat. He was only half joking, and you could see the thought of the one thing his heart ached for the most – a thought he couldn't act on – was weighing his soul down. He took a breath and shifted in his seat, then continued.

"Um, what do you miss? Just about everything." Bails tries to fight the tears welling up at this point. An impossible task, given he's just invoked the thought of his wife. He tries to distract himself with superficial details.

"Even just the drive to work – pretty casual drive, might pick up a red light maybe, drive along the beach... just everything. It becomes very emotional for me..."

His voice again crackles, and there's another pause.

"You know, you walk in and..." He pauses again, wiping at his eyes with embarrassment. "Because I love all the banter and the chats with the players, just the off chats that you might have when you run into someone are something you miss. It's not so much the routine; it's just the – you're not sure what's gonna happen next, you know? It's the people. Who's gonna train well? Who's gonna kick well? Who's gonna kick shit? Who's gonna be good at training?"

I was still stuck on his three word summary: *it's the people.*

What? I blinked, then nodded as if I was expecting that answer so I could buy time and consider what I'd just heard. Shouldn't it be the competition? The wins? The lights? The show? I came here to inspire the guys, not get some puff piece about friends.

I firmly believed — because I'd seen it play out with my own eyes — that to get ahead you needed to park relationships. The best performers can't give themselves to anyone else until they've carried out the essentially "selfish" task of perfecting their craft.

As Bails fiddled with his oxygen tube again, I was left to ponder: *Can you be a people person AND have the ultimate success?* I didn't have to reach far back into my own memory to find evidence.

Bails had sidled up to my office on occasion, before players arrived, while we both scoffed a coffee down after a morning workout.

"Tell me something new Paddy," was a common line on those mornings, usually delivered with a mouthful of muffin and a casual lean against the doorframe.

On one fresh morning during our first season together, as the Summer turned to Autumn, I had literally just finished a book that I knew would give him a buzz.

"You know how we were talking about the keys to success the other morning?" He nodded, the enthusiasm as much for the breakfast he was chewing on his as it was for the topic I raised.

"Well there's this book I just finished that highlighted all these famous guys who had one thing in common."

"Like who?" Bails probed between bites.

I carried on with my usual enthusiasm when sharing a psych summary with Bails. "Well, the whole book was about the answer that they found from a study with a future US President nicknamed JFK, 266 other men, and some surprising results about what really leads to success."

"JFK!" Bails was all in now.

"Yep, the great man himself. See, in the 30s, researchers from Harvard wanted to understand what determines good health rather than illness. They hoped they could help the US army select better officer candidates as they geared up for World War II. So they set out to answer a simple question: What predicted the best performers in life, when selecting from an already stellar field?"

Bails was nodding now, his silence an invite for me to keep going. So I did.

"The big point is simple," I cut to the chase. "What matters most in life is relationships."

"You mean the secret to people being happy and stuff?" Bails seemed a little deflated, thinking he was going to find a secret to success, not soft stuff.

"*Everything*," I replied, with extra weight. "They found that the things we all think predict success hardly mattered. Money and IQ didn't matter much. But when it came to relationships, the results were crystal clear. Success in relationships was a strong predictor of economic success *and* mental & physical health."

The numbers told an amazing tale, and I shared them with Bails – a numbers guy who loved a good stat – with gusto. I told him how not only were those with positive relationships and good people skills more likely to have higher life satisfaction and better mental health, but they were more successful too, earning more than twice that of the men with the worst scores for relationships on average. And the high scorers were also 3-times more likely to have professional success worthy of inclusion in Who's Who — in industries as cut-throat as publishing, medicine, war, and politics.

"Well I'll be, Paddy." Bails rattled his keys with a little smile growing on his face. "That's the perfect excuse to go get another coffee & work on our people skills. We'll be the most successful people in the building!"

I was snapped back to the room by a rattling cough that resulted from Bails trying to clear his throat.

I look up to see the typically dry, poker-faced coach close to tears again. My personal instincts compel me to reach out to him as his breathing becomes shallower. Like anchors though, my arms stay cemented to my sides, the training from years of dealing with those who are grieving overriding my human instincts to help the man in front of me.

"As you can see, it … um, impacts me a lot."

I fight the urge to hug him, and for a moment I catch myself asking why. "It starts and ends with people" – one of the first nuggets of wisdom Bails ever handed to me on a plate, along with a muffin over a coffee near the apartment we shared in Brighton – rings in my ears. For a moment, I ready myself to give him a man-hug.

He shifts in bed, the bed remote falls to the floor, and the moment is gone.

"Yeah, I can understand," I start to say, reaching to pick up the remote from the linoleum covered hospital room floor. Sterile and safe, like my non-emotive response to Bails' emotions. And then I reconsider what I've just said: "Well, I can't really understand, but I see what you're saying."

With that admission, I begin to wonder if I've gotten myself in over my head. I may have liked the idea of interviewing a man on his deathbed, but how on earth do I empathize at this point? I pray for a fire alarm or a phone call, or even a cheer from the tennis on TV to distract us and give us a chance to come up for air.

Luckily, Bails is too busy composing himself to have noticed my discomfort.

"No, as each day passes..." the pause draws out for a few more seconds as he composes himself with a couple of slow, deep breaths. Then another wave of tears begin.

"I'm not in a good way, and ah..."

The delay is excruciating now. Five seconds. Ten seconds. The silence hovers like the heat that greeted me on my arrival in the morning. Stifling and still.

"That's why I'm sort of putting some unnecessary pressure on you and Nick and Burgo to help my son."

I feel the need to reassure him here on something that isn't too hard.

"Please, don't hesitate about that – it's not unnecessary at all."

39

"Yeah well," he replied without thought, "It, it is. 'Cos if I wasn't crook I'd feel uncomfortable about doing it. Anyways, regardless of that, I trust you three blokes, and you just need to get him in – he's a loyal little prick. The other one's okay, he'll be all right."

As hard as it was for a healthy, single guy to empathize with a dying, married man, it wasn't much of a stretch for me to imagine myself in the seat of his two sons, Mitch or Darcy. I have a father. How would I be if my own dad was going through this? The lump in my throat returned with a vengeance, so I asked another question to avoid crying myself.

"How are they going?"

I saw the answer with my own eyes in a second, even if the audible response was quiet.

"Oh," Bails pauses and chokes again, this time taking a moment to breathe, wipe his eyes and compose himself. "They're going okay. As well as they can be."

As if the pile marked "prayers for those in over their head" were the top priority for angels at that moment, a doctor walks in unannounced.

"G'day doc, how are you going?"

For a moment, we both breathe easier. I make a mental note-to-self: bring some tissues next time.

Without knowing the perfection of his timing, the doctor launches into his clinical interview. "How are we going?"

"Oh," Bails goes along with the script, "not bad."

"Not bad is good," states the doctor. "How'd you cope with the fluids and stuff yesterday?"

"Oh yeah," Bails replies without switching modes, "I pissed an enormous amount out." He laughs to himself at the potentially inappropriate use of slang.

For the next couple of minutes, the doctor and patient proceed to play verbal tennis rally, exchanging short question for short answer. Ironically the only noise apart from their exchange is the background soundtrack of the tennis on TV. Standard chemo questions? Check. Sleep? Check. Bathroom? Check. Pain? A little bit.

"Okay. Keep eating, keep moving, we'll keep on top of the pain, and we'll see if we can get you better."

"Yep. Yep. Yep... and yep."

All three men in the room smile slight smiles. Just the corner of the mouth curling, but in unison, three quarter-smiles almost equal a whole grin. A small win for humanity.

Bails takes a moment to disconnect from the clinical assessment, reorient with the room, and tune back in to the topic at hand before the doctor visited.

"What was I saying? Before I...," he paused and then drove ahead, "before I started to weep?"

Caught off guard now, I scrambled for notes that weren't there. "You were just talking about Mitch and Darc. It's also..."

My mind wandered now, still fixated on the discussion about his chest. Was Bails okay with me hearing that? Had I overstayed my welcome on the first interview? Maybe I should've had something ready in line with the key lesson of Facilitation 101: Prepare with the End in Mind, also known as Create an Exit.

"Mate, it's been an hour now, so if you want me to go, just let me know soon, okay?"

"Nah," Bails replied, ignorant of conversational conventions right now. I had come to hear his story, and no amount of discomfort would short-circuit that now. "They're okay. I think Mitch has a better understanding of how serious it is. Darcy's just starting to..." he began, unsure of where his thoughts would lead right now. "I think at the start it was just, *'Oh well, dad's dad. He'll just come home.'* But I think in the last couple of weeks, Caron said he was starting to sort of ask a little bit more questions. You know, *'Dad was gonna come home, but now that he's not coming*

41

home, and he's in hospital...' Yeah he knows it's a bit more serious. He's becoming aware of the seriousness of it."

He turns his attention from his boys now, and focuses on the newest entry into his life: the cancer.

"The radiation I've had recently, to me – because I've got the lump in me – I feel like the radiation feels like it's having a bit of an impact on it."

"You can actually feel it?" I asked out of curiosity.

"Yeah, I can," he replied, matter of fact. "The lump's not as big. This morning Caron said, *'I think the lump's got a little bit smaller.'* But when you look at it every day, you know, sometimes you look at it and you can convince yourself: *'Shit, there's nothing there!'*"

He was reaching up and across with his right arm now, lifting his left arm so he could touch the foreign body that was protruding from his ribs.

"They gonna hit you again?" I ask.

"Yeah, they do it again. Over the next three weeks, I dunno whether I'll be able to get out of here or not though, 'cos I do take... it does take a little bit of care to look after me, so. For all I know, I could be in here for another three weeks while the treatment's going."

Intrigued, I started to map out the plan for the next few weeks. "So you do once a week for three weeks? Or you get three weeks off now?"

"One dose, then they track me, and, um, the next ones around about three weeks."

"Right." I nod as if I understand the magnitude of what he's talking about. In reality, I have no idea.

"So, they might make me stay a while Paddy. Better than a poke in the eye."

"That's a fair statement." I don't think it is, but I don't want to argue the point. Right now, I would pay someone to poke me in the eye if only it would mean I could leave the room.

42

"Correct. If you gotta go..."

Has he sensed my discomfort?

"I don't have to go," I clarify, "but I'm wary of wearing you out as well. I'll be coming back. Now that I know you're okay with it, I'll come back at least once a week. I'll give you a heads up by email. You still get your emails don't you?"

"Yeah, yeah, yeah."

Good. Emails and tangibles are some things I can control and prep. "I might shoot you a text or an email to say, 'Here's a couple of ideas I had to chat about,' so that way I don't catch you on the hop too much."

"Sounds all right."

"And yeah, if you, um..."

How do I leave it? I thought I'd take a leaf from the main point of the day: other people matter.

"From a support point of view, if you want fewer people, more people. I guess, whatever you want, just let us know."

I pause, then think of one other thing that might lift him. "And the thing with Mitch? It's a no-brainer. You don't even have to ask." The finish was better than the start.

"All right, that's good." Bails showed no smile, but his eyes suggested hope for two things. First and foremost, that his son would get the chance he wanted for him. And second, that these chats weren't going to be a waste of time after all. The two things he was a natural at in life – people and giving – had helped ease his pain, physical and emotional, at least for a moment.

"You gonna flick me his number?" I ask, picking up my phone to reconnect with the world.

"Yeah, you shoulda got it by now."

"Ah yeah," I reply, recalling Bails sending the details through. Flustered is an understatement right now. "Lemme check."

I check my phone, and a new contact sits on my home screen: Mitchell Bailey.

"Ok cool, I'll hit him up as soon as I walk out." I stand up and gather my things, relieved to see the Dictaphone still working away. "Or maybe after I grab another coffee first."

"Ha ha!" He laughs with his eyes this time. "Good to know some things don't change."

As I walk back out of the hospital and into the real world, I'm struck by the contrast between outside and inside. The blazing sunlight versus the dim fluorescent lighting. The noise of the nearby street versus the hush of the nearby corridor. The heat versus the climate controlled air.

For the most part though, I notice the normality of it all outside, versus the parallel, suspended universe for those inside. I flashed back to Bails sitting in bed, staring at the curtain rail. Just waiting.

The mixture of emotions involved in the whole situation, and the looming difficulty ahead – for Bails, for his family, for the players and coaches, and for me – begin to sink in. The tears welling in my eyes don't get high enough to spill onto my face, thanks to my phone buzzing, and I'm happy for the distraction. It was Bails.

I forgot to ask u about the house hunting.

I smiled and began tapping my response as I wiped my eyes and then reached for my car keys.

Ah, still a work in progress- going to check out a couple of options later today.

Good luck.

Typical of a man who was so in touch with people that he could still show interest in your life, even as his was falling apart.

Cheers mate.

In the comfort of the air-conditioned car as I drove away, I pulled over to make a note on the phone, so I didn't forget. In one visit — filled with jokes, stories about leadership, and even tears as he spoke about his boys — he had already opened my eyes. Bails helped me see a simple truth:

Performance starts with people.

Not sure what I intended to do with the note, I felt I should at least capture the essence of our first serious chat before I returned to the rat race. Another text came through just as I finished.

> Hi just missed you its Caron. Saw you driving out of the car park. Thanks for visiting x

SESSION 1 – TOUCH

| | | |

It's late 2013, and the players are between sessions: on- field training is done for the day, and weights don't start until after lunch. Some file in to see their line coach and dissect the video. Others are getting medical treatment in another part of the facility.

In Bails' office, there is a serious air as he motions for one of the players to close the door.

Coach sits back in his chair, hands behind his head, the whiteboard behind him covered with his daily bread and butter: football knowledge.

On the left, there is a neat row of magnets labeled with players' names, some accompanied by scribbled notes next to them. On another part of the board were one-word ideas & codenames that would've made sense when he was waxing about them to one of the other coaches. And in the middle, inside the boundary lines of a drawn up playing-field, a spaghetti dish of lines and arrows that represented running patterns for players.

Bails' brow had almost as many lines on it, making it clear that his laid back posture wasn't one of relaxation. His level of concern matched the dramatic tone of his voice as he shook his head in exasperation.

"This is unacceptable."

Two players perched opposite him – Truck, the big burly veteran full back, fills the chair on the other side of Bails' desk. Sloaney leans casually against the window.

Both of them hold positions of huge influence in the team. Truck was the most experienced player on the list, and as such, carried the *weight of years behind him whenever he spoke. Sloaney was a star on the rise, already hailed as an emotional leader within the environment.*

A small grin appeared at the side of Truck's mouth as he nods in agreement.

"We can't have them bringing down the neighbourhood," he concurs, looking at Sloaney for his two- cents.

Sloaney takes the cue: "That's why we thought we would bring it to the Council meeting."

"And as Mayor of Brighton," Bails decreed with as much pomposity as he could muster, "I'm glad you did. You've done well, my young padawan."

They all chuckle and the meeting is underway.

The unofficial Brighton City Council – headed by Bails, and supported by fellow residents of Adelaide's affluent suburb of Brighton – would meet on a casual basis every other week. There was no formal agenda prepared, and no set time chiseled into the weekly schedule. But when the big guy and his blonde sidekick both happened to be in Bails' office at the same time, they all knew what business was at hand.

On this occasion, the topic of conjecture was immigration – in particular the whispers of two potential new residents from within the team. A star player and a prominent coach were both asking questions about life in Brighton.

"What worries me is their motive." Bails leans forward from his reclined position, clasping his hands in front of him as he perched his elbows on his desk. "Are they in it for the title? Or because they actually belong on the better side of the Boulevard?"

"We-hell," Sloaney exhaled, "I think we all know the answer to that one."

"You don't need to be a rocket scientist, do you?" Truck, almost as quick with the dry wit as Bails, prompted a round of laughter.

"Order!" Bails banged his fist on the desk mockingly, lifting the laughter to a crescendo before it settled again.

A trainer walks past, glancing through Bails' office window with a quizzical look on his face. Chuckles all round again inside the council chambers, and they agree on a council strategy. They will be subtle, dropping enough hints in an attempt to dissuade the immigrants from settling in their little slice of Adelaide. With no other matters raised, the Council was adjourned.

They slipped out from the council chambers that doubled as Bails' office, rejoining the steady hum of noise and movement typical of any football club. Barely a soul noticed the exchange that had just taken place.

But in a few short minutes, between reps, recovery, and reviews, a bond had grown between players and coach. No knowledge needed to change hands – just a simple game of role play, where the coach became an actor alongside the players. An equal, just for the fun of it.

SESSION 2
STRETCH
WE TALK ABOUT MENTORING & GROWTH

Before heading back in to visit Bails again, I decided I needed some help to make sure I could handle what might come up.

Mark Purser, or simply "the Rev," as most of the guys tagged him when he was around the team, was a genial guy in his forties who was altogether average in much of his appearance. Average height, well groomed and polite, Mark was someone you could bet your house on, who had never been accused of being either over or under dressed. A little like Bails insofar as that, at first glance, there wasn't anything that jumped out.

It was once a conversation started, however, that the Rev was clearly different from Bails. Effervescent, bubbly, and always willing to empathize or agree, Mark was initially a little overwhelming for some of the players and staff when he first started at the Crows.

He and Bails hit it off well though, partly due to Dean's past experiences with a club chaplain at Melbourne. So much so, that Mark was one of the few people Dean and Caron really leaned on as they bunkered down for the fight of their lives.

Which is how I came to know – not straight from the source, but via a simple phone call from the Rev – that Caron had loved the idea when Dean told her about the *Breakfast With Bails* plan.

Knowing the Rev specialised in this sort of thing, and given that I hadn't handled the first visit as well as I'd have liked, I peppered him with questions while I had him on the line: how do you deal with that level of emotion? How do you help them stay positive? How do you help them find their paths if things are looking so bleak that others might give up?

Willing to help as always, Rev happily described what he thought he gave to people in this situation: hope. Not false hope, but an acceptance of reality, while still thinking there might be something in it for them.

"I mostly just ask questions," Rev explained. "I don't tell, don't force it – and help them find something they believe in. Sometimes that's based on faith; sometimes on more earthly things."

With some sound guidance on how to tackle this level of depth, I took a metaphorical breath and decided I was all-in.

In between meetings the next day, I checked to see if Thursday – our last scheduled day off for January – would work for our next "training session."

Up for breakfast Thursday Bails?

The response came back in a short time, typically staccato and to the point:

Paddy- Campo at 10am. 10.30am for u.
Text me first as my last two mornings have
been very rough.

Before leaving my office for the next video session, I tapped back a reply:

Ok, mate will do.

While it was in front of my mind, I pondered the promise I'd made to him when we first set out on the project to email or text topics ahead of time, so he had time to consider his answers.

More time to think meant less likelihood of clichéd answers Bails was so well trained at giving when caught off guard by a curly question during a press conference.

Without too much thought, I grabbed a pen and paper and set out to induce a "brain vomit" – an outpouring of thoughts and ideas without any critique of their quality. "Get it all out and tidy it up later," Bails had remarked when I told him about this technique. "I like it."

After a few minutes, I sat back and checked the list. Some huge themes, and possibly a little scarier than both Bails or I may be able to handle at this stage.

With a little bit of scribbling and crossing out, I reduced the monster list down to a starting point at least. Those that made the first cut I typed into a text message and flicked it to Bails.

> Hey mate just a heads up on the q's I
> wanted to ask during the next visit:
> What do you reckon football
> teaches you about life?
> What have you seen it teach guys
> you have coached?
> What has it taught you that
> you're drawing on now?
> Don't have to answer anything you don't
> want to obviously, and if half hour of
> Campo's laugh wears you out
> just lemme know & we'll do
> another time - P

With any luck, I tell myself, these might open up doorways to bigger conversations on life and death and everything else cancer would make you think about.

51

"Oh, I'm a bit better." Bails definitely didn't look better than the last time I saw him; his eyes were puffier, and tiredness dampened his every gesture. "Yeah, bit better this morning. Last couple of days haven't been great."

"Is that 'cos of the treatment?"

At first he doesn't acknowledge the question, too busy adjusting himself on the bed. Brow furrowed, he sits forward and adjusts the pillows, then the bed height and the position of the tubes around him. For a moment, I'm unsure if he is going to answer. Eventually, he does.

"Not getting any sleep, more than anything." The annoyed expression on his face fits, although I'm unsure if the comfort of the bed is still his main concern as opposed to the lack of sleep. He answers my next question without me even having to ask.

"Can't get any sleep. This little backpack sorta just... that's the morphine that's getting sent into me. And that gets changed every twenty-four or every twenty-two hours actually, and unfortunately they've organised it, so it gets changed at 3 or 4 in the morning. So that doesn't help."

"Just as you're drifting off, hey?"

"3 o'clock in the morning they're waking me up to change it and play with it. That's before the sparrows have even thought about farting."

No wonder he's worn down – his environment was conspiring against him, corralling him into playing the game of life on someone else's terms.

I decide to take his mind off the frustrations of being cooped up in an oppressive environment for a bit. "I just caught up with Mitch."

"Yep?" My attempt at rousing some curiosity works, and he sits still for the first time since I've been in the room today.

"Spoke to him about how I think there might be..." I catch myself, and re-word to emphasise that this is serious. "Actually, I think there IS, 'cos I want to but can't do it myself – there's a need

52

for a program coordination kind of role that mixes a bit of injury prevention stuff, from a physical and ex-physiology point of view, with what we're doing from a technical retraining point of view."

I use Jake Kelly as an example. Jake is the son of former Collingwood star defender Craig Kelly, who we managed to pick up at the tail end of the draft thanks to a kicking style that had made every other team flinch and turn elsewhere. Just like quarterbacks and pitchers and shooters, the mechanics of kickers make a real difference - only in our game, *everyone* had to be able to kick.

"We know from video breakdown when he kicks that he's tight here, here and here." I point to various parts of the body as I go. "So we've given him these focus points and exercises and stuff. But then at the same time, the physios and docs, from an injury prevention point of view, they've given him a set of stretches and things to potentially address the same issues."

One thing that appealed to our scouts about Jake as we went through the recruiting process was his mentality: there was no doubt that whatever he was given, he would do at 100 percent. Within a week of first arriving after the draft, he had already earned the nickname "Bull" from his new teammates, thanks to his bull-at-a-gate style in every single warm up drill.

"We just need to make sure it's all on the same page and being coordinated," I continued. "Like we always talk about, the structure we put around the kid should help guide his behaviour and channel his drive, so we just need to make sure all the walls are facing the same way, if that makes sense."

Bails nodded, and I moved back to his eldest son.

"From Mitch's point of view, I think he can help us with that."

I watch for a reaction from Bails while I explain the idea, hoping for an indication of his pleasure or otherwise at what he's hearing. He hocks a massive loogey and spits into his vomit bag.

He coughs, and then looks back at me. He's listening intently, and I can almost see him mentally arranging the pieces in his mind, trying to work out where Mitch would fit.

"So for him," Bails probed, "what does that mean he does?"

I attempt to sum it up for him in twenty-five words or less. "He'd be bridging the gap across a little bit of the football specific stuff, and a little bit of injury prevention."

"So it's a real opportunity?" Bails asks. "Its not a Mickey Mouse..."

"Nah, I wanted it done and just didn't have time myself."

" Okay."

"All he needs," Bails pauses to spit into his bag again, "unfortunately, he just needs to improve his communication skills. He just needs to be a bit more social with people. He knows his stuff, he's a highly intelligent kid but he's a bit short with the explanation. *'Why don't you know it?'* – there's a little bit of that about him. *'You should know this, it's in your interests to know this sort of thing.'*"

He coughs and then continues.

"It'll lead to something. I just want him to have the chance, that's all. I've asked you for the favor, and Nick, and I'm gonna ask Burgo for the favor as well. Once he gets his foot in the door, he'll be as loyal as anything. I know that. He just needs someone to open the door for him and say 'come in' and 'I'll give you a hand.' Someone who believes in him and ... He'll put the hours in, no doubt about that.'"

I nod as he pauses for breath, takes a sip of water and then almost immediately is spitting into the bag again.

" Okay," his eyebrows relax, and he puts his spit-bag down again, happy to return to his previous obsession. "Nah, this morning wasn't too bad. I try to get to sleep about quarter past ten, and then I'm awake a few times a night. I almost have to lay stiff."

"'Cos you got your tubes in?"

"Yeah, I don't wanna pull them out while I am asleep, is one thing... I'm lying here stiff thinking *'If I move, and I get a bit sore and it'll aggravate me a little bit'* and I sort of need to move around a little bit to be honest."

"Do you wanna go for a walk?" I offer as he shifts himself on the edge of the bed again.

"I was gonna suggest we just go for a bit of a stroll." His eyes seemed to light up a little, but that could've been my imagination. "It's only gonna be to the end of the hall and back a couple of times for now, that's all," he told me, making sure I didn't get my hopes up. "Nothin' special, just to get a bit of the oxygen moving around in me." He pushed the table that held his sick bag away a bit and leaned forward, swinging his legs around so he could stand.

"Better take my little... bag of tricks with me!" He grinned, more of a grimace, really, as he reached for the bag on the table. "Where is this fucking thing?" he muttered in frustration a moment later, fiddling with the straps on the bag. It's the first time I've seen his anger with the whole situation come to the surface.

"You got it?" I started to reach for it, but he found the elusive buckle even as I asked.

"Yeah, I'll carry it." He firmed up his grip, and we headed for the door. Before I can ask about how frustrated he's getting being cooped up in his room, he takes the lead on the conversation.

"I get to see your brother a lot more often on the TV now," he said as we walked past the television in the corner. "It's like he's got me trapped."

I nodded, ushering him into the corridor. My younger brother, Tom, was moving up in the national news scene, and fast. "Yeah, his career's going great guns right now – he's filling in on the breakfast show over the summer, plus he's recording some new crime show, and back reporting news in Sydney. No more *Current Affair* stuff."

We strolled up the hallway at a sedate pace past doors open, and doors closed.

"Yeah," I continued, "he's flying. I was saying to someone the other day, it used to be when we were younger that Tom was always the brother of Carl or the brother of Paddy." Our older brother Carl had also had a career as a player in the AFL, more successful than mine. "Nowadays we are the brothers of Tom."

Raising both eyebrows, Bails quipped, "Sibling rivalry, eh?"

"Nah," I denied, "just a funny story. I'm pumped for him." That wasn't a lie - I was proud of my brother, excited for his success. "I'll admit it didn't make sense to me when he picked it as a career – the rest of us are in sciences or sports or economics or architecture – but it's what he loves. I don't know why he loves it, but that doesn't really matter, does it?"

"Mmm." I smiled at the skepticism packed into that tiny, noncommittal noise.

"We have damn good arguments sometimes, though – back and forth on the text messages for hours, some days – about the merits of the media." Reaching the end of the hall, we turned around, and I nodded toward Bails. "I think it was after your suspension, and I wrote to him 'the media are assholes.' He responded with the typical media line of *'We're giving the viewers what they want to see'*, I went back with 'What about the lives of those people involved', and we were off."

Passing by an open room – at our angle, only the foot of a bed and a vase of cheery sunflowers was visible – Bails paused. The last line touched a nerve for him. "What did he say to that?"

I shrugged. "Well, the long and the short of it was, he says that these days it's the job of reporters to get as many people to watch or read their stuff as they can. That's how the media makes a living, how they get their wins." We started walking again. "Dunno how that gives any sense of meaning to the journo – seems superficial to me."

"Yeah," Bails nodded, "but I suppose for him, it's just about being the best, and the first. Kind of like us – some people might argue kicking a ball around isn't that important either."

I winced. "Touché. But I sometimes wonder, how long can you live in that world that's a little short on meaning without getting over it?" We turned again, started back toward the far end. "It's fun for a bit, but surely you need to have some sense of purpose or higher meaning in your work?"

"For sure."

"What was it for you?" I asked him. "How did you find meaning in a job... in an industry... that can be a bit superficial and fast food at times?"

He smiled, looking back through his memories as his pace slowed a bit.

"Ahh... the best thing for me was watching a young guy grow and develop." He smiled slightly; I don't think he was even aware of it. "Nothing better than seeing a young boy – 'cos that's still what they are when they turn up, eighteen-year-old boys, straight out of high school – grow into a man who can make good decisions for himself. It starts with a ball, and a patch of grass, but then it seeps, it drips into the rest of their lives as well." He looked over at me to make sure I was paying attention.

"The other day I ran into a young fella I had coached a few years back, and you know the best thing he said to me?" I shook my head. "He told me about something that I remembered teaching him when he was fresh in the game." He smiled again, this time completely aware of it. "To know that I had taught him something and that it had stuck, and he'd now grown up and could do it... Yeah, the best part of coaching is watching and helping young players grow, on and off the field. There's nothing like it."

We fell into a companionable silence, each thinking our own thoughts – me about my brother and Bails about his players over the years – as we turned at the end of the corridor one last time.

Everything was so quiet as if we were the only ones there. Or at least the only ones awake.

"So I suppose," I said slowly, a little reluctant to break that silence, "there's something like that for media folk, too."

"Great people and the right environment are vital for anyone who's pursuing excellence." Such a simple statement, but it struck me how easily he had nailed the essence of the chat right there. Bails cocked his head to the side. "He's got the trifecta, then?"

I frowned. "The trifecta?"

"Yeah – he's found what he loves, he's good at it, and he has people around him who believe in him. That's the sweet spot in life."

"Yeah." I nodded my agreement and grinned at Bails. "That's a good way of putting it."

As though that was some sort of signal, he pushed back into his room and I followed. He headed straight for the bathroom. "Just sit tight mate," he told me, gesturing towards the chair I'd used earlier with one hand, gripping the edge of the bathroom door with the other. "I just gotta see if I can get a win over these drugs by taking a crap..."

I sat as the door clicked shut and began to go through my notes, jotting down a couple of thoughts from our stroll about the halls, and noting a memory it had bought up from when times were more normal.

"Think I got an answer for you, Bails," I spoke loud enough so he could hear me over the shower in the coaches' locker room.

Unlike the player's space this was a smaller, tighter area. Thanks to having only one toilet and one shower for the football staff, it often forced interactions and chats while we waited for workmates to finish their business. Some were superficial. Others were fruitful.

This one in particular was a day after Bails had posed a question in a coaches meeting: *How can we, as coaches, make sure we keep those on the 'fringe' motivated and engaged?* I'd wrestled with his question overnight.

"Oh yeah?" Bails had appeared around the edge of the stall, beginning to dry himself off. Like most conversations in sports locker rooms, the fact he was naked as we talked didn't stop the conversation for a second.

"It actually reminded me of this story I read about the guy that built the first iPhone." I was getting dressed too, picking up my phone as I mentioned it.

This prompted a raised eyebrow from Bails as he pulled his navy blue team polo shirt over his head. "The old iPhone, hey?"

"Yep," I took the lead and dived into the story. "One of the key guys on the initial project was named Kirk Phelps." I went into storytelling mode as we finished getting dressed now, describing to Bails how Phelps had experienced a unique style of teaching at college.

"He was groomed in a computer science program at Stanford that seems so mechanical from the outside," I relayed the story that I had re-read the night before. "But those who go through it rave about one man: Ed Carryer, who fills his students in his 'Smart Product Design' class with belief."

As we left the locker room and walked passed our offices to get a coffee, we talked about how the same environment existed at Apple too.

"The common thread between that class and working for Apple was they both allowed them to play," I explained to Bails, "to explore their talents, and to work as a team to create something they believe is great. In both places, people made irrational sacrifices, working incredibly hard because they believed."

"Yeah," Bails dug into his own bag of experience. "I think belief's got such a big thing to do with it for our guys. If they don't believe they can win, or even change, they're gonna struggle. Belief's the difference between just missing and just winning, I reckon."

I went a little further with his example. "Did you know that when people feel their leader believes in them, they work harder, and perform better? It's called the Pygmalion effect."

"Dunno about the name, Paddy, but I do believe that." He nods as he placed our standard order. "I also believe this coffee is going to do wonders for my edits this morning."

I smiled and agreed, keen to get back to work myself. It could have been the coffee or the company, but I always felt like working a little harder after a one of these chats.

I didn't know how much time had passed since Bails went to the restroom. A few minutes perhaps, but I hadn't looked at my iPhone. The door opened.

"How'd you go?" I asked as Bails returned from the toilet and slowly made his way back to his bed.

"Ah, yeah... just wheezing all the time." He sat, scooting back a bit but making no effort to swing his legs up. "That's not great but... it's also part of the treatment as well. A little side effect." " He grimaced, huffing a small laugh.

"A side effect 'cos the healthier lung cells are struggling?"

"I think what happens is that the, ah, pleural lining in my lungs is where the cancer is." Looking down at the bed, he plucked at the bed sheet, pulling it out from under his left leg before looking up at me again. "It's starting to spread. Like, as you can see, I've got a tumor hanging out the side here." He glanced down toward his side at a bit of a bulge beneath his hospital gown. "It was bigger, but it's got smaller because the radiation's affecting it. It's reducing it a little bit – not by much, but it's affecting it." Having never seen the tumor in question before now, I couldn't judge for myself. I did feel a pang in my own chest though.

"You were saying that last time," I reminded him as I shifted in my seat to distract from the discomfort, "that Caron thinks it's a bit smaller, but not the doctor?"

"Yeah, the doc checks and says, *'Oh, it looks okay...'*" He shrugged. "Only yesterday did he look and go, *'Nah, that is – it is smaller.'* We've looked at it, and we've identified that it's smaller." Shaking his head, he continued, "One of the hardest things is to keep the weight on. It's eating."

My eyebrows jumped up all on their own at that. "You're not hungry? You!?"

"I'm hungry, don't worry!" he laughed. "But the food..." He gave a dramatic shudder. "The food's crap. It's just ridiculous."

"I'll have to smuggle some of the sweet stuff in next time then," I told him with a smile. Bails' had a sweet tooth as big as his head.

"Well, I've got Caron--," a cough interrupted him, phlegmy and wet, but brief. "I said to Caron to bring some fruit salad in, all that kind of stuff, 'cos I can just – I'm not gonna eat all day, but I can have a bit every now and then."

"I just drove past her on the way here, actually! She on her way to the shops or something?"

Bails nodded. "Yeah, I said to her to just bring me a little bit of something. I've got a little fridge in there, as you know, and I can't eat the chocolate 'cos it gets all thick and mucousy in my throat. Um, you know, like yesterday I had a choice of three things, and I chose something I thought would be all right, and then when it arrived I was like *'Nah, I can't eat that.'*" His forehead wrinkled a bit as he tried to remember the offending food. "Maaa... Meatloaf!" was his triumphant conclusion.

He shrugged again. "I'm gonna have to get Caron to get me a tin of apricots. Just so I can eat them when I want them, not just at that time and that time, which they dictate to me."

In here, Bails had no autonomy. He was definitely not in control of the battle against the cancer. And he was disconnected from his purpose. If all three together make great people grow, I didn't want to think about what happens when none of the three are present.

He shifted again, bringing his back up against the raised head of the bed and lifting his legs so he could stretch them out flat. Pushing his head into the pillow, he closed his eyes.

"I'm on constant morphine, so that plugs me up. And it's funny... My feet though, they go a bit scaly... This one here," he waggled his right foot toward me. "I clipped my toes the other day, and this one here I clipped and just cut the skin a tiny bit. Only a small mark, but from there, 'cos the chemo is smashing my immune system, that toe's no good." I checked: the toe in question did look pretty awful.

"But my mum and dad are over, so Mum'll probably come in about one and give them a rub. That's her job. She said '*I'll be in, and I'll give you a massage.*' So I said '*You do that, love.*' So she's gonna massage the guts out of my feet, God love her." He drew his feet back in under the sheet.

"They came in yesterday, you said?" That was good to hear; he should have his family nearby.

"Yeah, got in yesterday. Drove over from Melbourne in a caravan."

"They brought a caravan over?"

"Yeah," he said with a bemused smile, "they bought a caravan, staying in a caravan park. It's only down the road from our joint in Brighton, so they could've stayed there, but I think mum likes to have a bit of her own time. And I think Caron likes my mum having her own time."

We both laugh at that. It's not that his wife and his mum butt heads, but everyone needs a little privacy now and then.

"Anyway, you want a chewy?" He points to a small sack on the windowsill beside a potted plant someone had brought to give the room a bit of colour.

"Yeah, okay," I accept the offer, mindful of coffee breath.

Shoving over onto his side, he stretched out until he could snag a corner of the sack and pull it toward him. "Now these are special, so I can only give you one..." he said, giving the bag a bit of a shake. Two of the candies drop into my outstretched hand.

"Oh, no!" I said in mock horror. "You gimme two!"

"Oh, shit," Bails laughed. "I'm outta control." I started to hand one of them back, but he waved me off. "Take it. My mum bought these – she handed them over, and it was like she was giving me ... you know, a thousand dollars or something, and she says, *'These are really, really... really, really, really good these.'* And I've gone, 'Oh, all right.' To me they're just chewy mints."

He slowly unwrapped the chewy, mimicking his mother. "So as she hands them over, she opens another one. *'They're yours,'* she says, *'they're really good,'* and then she takes her share. Which she's notorious for." I laughed a little at that. Like mother, like son? He popped the chewy into his mouth.

"Yeah," he chewed for a moment, then started up again. "So they're over for about a week or so. What else is going on? What's going on at the club? What's not going well? How are our new goalposts going?" We had come up with an idea together to use smaller target areas after our respective end of season trips, and it was a pet project of his just before he had to come to hospital.

"They'll be up in about a week, I think," I told him. "So that's goin' well. They're just starting to talk about, in the box, that Nobes is gonna fill in for you to start." I leaned forward in my chair, keen to tap into his experience in the hot seat. "What was your most important role on gameday?"

He didn't have to think about it long. "Whether the other coaches like it or not, they all commentate at some stage. They get caught up in the game too much sometimes." He paused for a moment, considering his words. "They're watching the game. They become... what is it?" He frowned, unable to find the word he searched for.

"Blind?" I supplied. "They lose situational awareness. So the coach's job is to provide the head coach with that, so he can provide the players with it."

"Yeah," Bails nodded, relaxing a bit.

"And when you're commentating," I finish the thread, "you're not helping the next person in the chain to be aware of that."

"Exactly. I've got no doubt that what I would've done more this year," Bails continues, "was just pull the coaches in a little bit as they were starting to get a bit carried away." I must've looked confused or something, because he hurried to explain. "What I mean by that is, they say things like 'Oh God, here we go' and 'Oh shit, he's gonna miss this kick.' They just need to control their concentration a bit, you know? This is about just trying to get the basics out rather than commentating or giving an opinion on everything. 'Cos we could be playing shithouse for thirty seconds and then we're great again."

"So is it a bit like what we just said about Bull," I suggested, "you gotta put the right things around them to point their talents and their focus in the right direction?"

"Yes!" He agreed with ample enthusiasm. Bails was right in the groove now, and he carried on dishing out advice on how to coach, how we should prep the team, and how to guide talented people. Talking football, and performance in general, was something he would do underwater with a mouth full of marbles. The only thing that stopped him now after about five minutes was a deep cough that wracked his body. He sat in silence after he had cleared his throat of the mucous again, perhaps a little gun shy to carry on.

I took the silence like a gap in between defenders, and changed tack to a deeper topic. "So did you get my questions that I sent through?"

"Yeah."

"Did they make sense to 'ya?"

"Oh, yeah. It was a text, wasn't it?" He frowned. Reaching under his pillow, he pulled out a cell phone and began scrolling through his texts until he found the one I'd sent him the other day. Reading through it again, he said, "Yeah... Yeah, they seem okay." I heard something large and wheeled roll down the corridor, but it turned off before getting much closer. "Ha ha. Yeah, Campos' laugh is pretty full on. *'What does football teach you about life?'* Jesus, Paddy." He looked over at me, one eyebrow raised. "That's a big question, asking someone who's dying in a fuckin' hospital room." Chuckling, Bails took another sip of water and stared out the window, thinking.

"Maybe if I put it a different way," I offered. "What do you learn from football? What does a kid learn from the game that he needs to learn?"

"Ah. I've always thought what you learn out of footy is the competition, to be honest. You learn how to compete. You learn how to lose. You learn how to win, but I think you also learn how to lose. You learn to evaluate yourself more. Sport gives you a chance to self-evaluate, even though you might not think you are doing it." He glanced my way to see if I was paying attention.

"What about for coaches?"

"Yeah dunno," Bails was honest, never pretending to know more than he did. "I don't know. The relationships you build with the players, I've always thought that they're so important. You gotta make it easy, you know. If you build that trust, that belief, they'll hang in there a bit longer with you. Bit like life."

I nodded.

"They've almost got a booster button on the back that you gotta press, and you just gotta press the green one as often as you can. Every now and then, you gotta press the red one to stop 'em, you know. But if you have to keep pressing it, then you gotta' think to yourself, *'Well I'm attacking this the wrong way. I can't get through to him.'* Or, *'He's not listening,'* or you gotta' do something a bit different. It's not about what makes you look good as a coach or even the player. It's about what works."

Focus on the positives, on what works, I scribbled. I was about to ask another question when a knock sounded on the door, and two of the more positive people in our entire organisation came bouncing in the room.

"Come in!" Bails called out as they did, still buzzing from the talk of his passion.

Rory Sloane – or Sloaney to fans and friends alike –pushed the door open a crack and peeked in before opening it all the way. He and Senior Assistant Coach Mark Bickley – or Bicks – came in together.

I stood with a smile. "Look out, here they are!"

"Hey, guys," Sloane said with a brief wave. The effervescent winger with the flowing blonde hair of a surfer, he also had a boyish smile that was ever present, and always infectious.

If Sloaney was effervescent, Bicks was a bubbling brook. So it was no surprise that they both launched into conversation with the same energy.

"How are 'ya, mate?" Both the new visitors ask Bails the same question at the same time, and I laughed as I looked at Bicks.

"Looking sharp, man," I told him. "You didn't have to get that dolled up for a hospital." He had ditched the standard coaching work wear of shorts and polo shirt for the day, and now wore a suit and dress shoes with neatly combed hair. Not something you saw every day inside the clubrooms.

"Ah nah," he said a bit sheepishly. "I've gotta go to something after this."

"You got another gig, don't you?" Bails accused. "Another gig!"

Bicks laughed. "Ha ha. Nah, I've just got..."

"There's no days off for Bicks!" I interrupted. "Another day, another thousand dollars!"

"I've gotta go see my accountant and do my tax," Bicks shook his head. "Very boring."

"I thought you mighta been dressed up for a sponsor's special deal or something," Sloane chimed in.

Bails looked from Sloane to Bicks to me and then back at Bicks. "Toyota?" he asked. Toyota had been a sponsor of our team from the start, and was almost as synonomous with the Crows as the town of Adelaide.

"Nah, tax," Bicks repeated. "I've got a new partner in crime on the Toyota sponsorship wagon." He nodded toward Sloaney.

"Is that right?" I asked Sloan. "Contract extras?"

He shook his head. "No extras, just..."

"Just out of the goodness of your heart?" Bails asked caustically.

"Charity work," Sloaney muttered, and we all laughed.

And without skipping a beat, the four of us slipped straight into regular banter mode as if death wasn't even in the room.

| | | |

The first week of pre-season training brings a unique energy to a football club.

Smiles and jokes abound as everyone trades stories of holiday, adventure, and bravado. A nervous energy is almost palpable among the players as they go through their testing. Anticipation is the main flavour for the coaches, as they find out how well their boys have kept in shape over the break.

In the midst of it all, a calm Bails sits in his office with Dave Mackay.

"What I wanna know, D-Mac, is in what are you good? What are your strengths?"

D-Mac was a reliable seventh-year player whose performance had plateaued the previous year. He sat attentive on the other side of the desk, not responding at first. He was a humble guy, and he wasn't used to talking himself up. Plus, the question was unusual.

Up until now, most chats with coaches were about what he needed to improve, or where he had gone wrong on the weekend and what he needed to change so that he could play better. He looked at the floor while he formulated his answer.

"I've got something I want you to try," Bails filled the silence with a statement, mobbing on with the question unanswered.

"Ok," D-Mac responded, grateful he didn't have to suffer through talking about his strengths. "I'm up for anything."

Bails leaned forward so that his sincerity was clear.

"Every day when you get in the car to come to training, I want you to drive a different way."

He let the suggestion sit in silence, as he watched the young man in front of him take it in. "So you're never going the same way twice."

The corner of his mouth turning up, D-Mac looked at Bails to check he was serious. He was. And he was about to hear why.

"Here's what I've seen from the first twelve months that I've been here," Bails declared. "I figured out that you're a pretty well-structured person." D-Mac nodded with slight hesitation, hoping to prompt Bails to go on. Instead, he went back to his first question.

"What are your strengths as a footballer?"

Having had time to think, and now more comfortable with the direction of the conversation, D-Mac volunteered two easy ones: run and carry. A wingman's bread and butter.

"Yes and yes," Bails agreed. "The thing that we are going to try to work on is your strengths as a player and how you can bring them out every week. I want you to look for ways to get involved in the game and use those strengths as much as you can, which is why I want you to think outside the box."

"Now your structure is a good thing in some areas, but that structure probly isn't helping your football too much. In an unpredictable offense, it's hard for you to break your old patterns."

D-Mac was nodding with more conviction now, and leaned forward himself. Bails continued his explanation, but now with more expression and movement.

"I want you to be more creative and explore your creative side. If you do things a bit different in your life, in the end it will help your football as well."

Again, D-Mac sat mute across the desk, this time not in surprise at what he heard, though, but because it seemed so spot on that there was no need to add anything. And so simple.

"So just drive a different way?" He enquired, checking he wasn't missing something.

"That's the first step," Bails smiled. "Next week I'll get you to brush your teeth with your left hand. And something different again after that. Hell, I'll have you coming into work in crazy Hawaiian shirts soon."

They both laughed, and Bails got up to open the office door, indicating the formal meeting was over.

"I'll be hot on you though," Bails warned as he walked past him and back into the hum of the rest of the football department.

As he walked away, D-Mac smiled to himself. As far as advice from a coach went, it was a little bit outside the square, a little bit different, but it resonated well with him.

It wasn't all about football – that is why that chat meant more to him than hundreds of others he'd had over the last seven years.

CONTACT
WE TALK ABOUT COMMUNITY & CONFIDENCE

Back at the coalface, the machine that is a professional football team rolled on without too much change. Coaches met, staff prepped, players trained, medicos treated. The only tangible difference in those first couple of weeks was Bails' empty office chair, which sat as a reminder of his absence each time I walked past. And the fact that my office was right next to his meant I had no option but to walk past. A lot.

As luck would have it, I was surprised to find an unexpected distraction in Jacob – one of Bails' favourite people at the club – sitting there one of the first times I walked past.

Jacob Milbank is one of the most popular employees at the Crows. A young man who wears his heart on his sleeve, he takes pride in the small jobs. And, when he is in a good mood, in doing them to the letter. Add to that his infectious smile and trademark low-key response when asked how he is - he would answer "not bad" if his pants were on fire - and he is one of the most welcome faces in the locker room each week, prompting from the players the same responses to his presence whether we were winning or losing. This unique gift alone makes him different from most employees.

Jacob is different for another reason as well – he has Down Syndrome, which makes him a true rarity in a professional sports team in Australia.

Today, Jacob was sad. And as always, he let everybody know it with his body language and an almost imperceptible volume when he answered my question about what was up.

"I'm sad about Bails," he murmured in response to my inquiry, without looking up from the desk. He lifted his left arm and – still not looking up – pointed limply to the hook on the wall. Still hanging there were two essential tools Bails took with him every time he stepped on the track during the summer. "I'm looking at his hat, and his whistle, and it makes me sad."

"Do you want to tell him something? Maybe you can write Bails a message on the whiteboard, and we can take a photo and I'll text it to him."

He looked up at me with red eyes. They began to smile at the idea.

"Yeah," he said, with a little more volume this time.

"Yeah, let's do that Jacob. What do you want to say?" I grabbed the whiteboard marker and rubbed off some X's and O's Bails had scribbled on one-half of the whiteboard and prepared to start writing.

"Bails," he began, deliberate and intense in his dictation.

"I miss you. Don't want you to pass away."

I hesitated – Jacob was transfixed on the marker as it brought his words to life, and I didn't want to let him fall back into the sad state I had found him now that we had gotten this far. I wrote what he said word for word, but then tried to redirect the message to finish on a positive.

"Maybe something about what you look forward to seeing when he comes back?"

"Yeah. Looking forward to you coming back."

"Yeah good, Jacob. He'll love that. You want to sign it?"

"You can do it," he suggested. "Make sure you write 'from Ledge.'" This was the nickname Bails always used when talking to Jacob – short for Legend.

I finished and stepped back so Jacob could see. He asked me to read it out, and once he was satisfied that it was right, he smiled his full, cherubic smile again.

"Now take a picture," he demanded, lifting his arm to give a thumbs up in preparation.

I took my phone out and snapped a pic. Checking the text in the background, glad that it was barely legible from a distance, I loaded up the pic along with a text message that I tinkered with:

> Jacob wanted me to send you this: "Bails, I miss you. I'm sitting in your office. Looking forward to you coming back. From Ledge."

Jacob was happy and he returned to work. I stood and stared at the message on the whiteboard after he left Bails' office, contemplating erasing the message. Before I could decide, the phone buzzed with a reply from Bails.

> He is a good man Jacob. Keeping the seat warm.

Glad he had received it well, I followed up with some locker room humor.

> Yeah, extra warm actually- he farted while we were there

The response was instant and deadpan.

> That's okay.

I erased the message on the whiteboard, keen to avoid others in the environment having their thoughts drift to the unthinkable. We all had a job to do, and Bails had already said to more than a few of us he wanted us to press on as if nothing was happening.

I had arranged to see Bails a few days later, and true to form he sent me a reminder on the way to the hospital.

> Paddy, as an entrance fee, can you bring a
> pizza roll from bakers delight ?

I chuckled and tapped a quick reply.

> Can do, big guy

Once I had picked up the supplies, I let him know, to build the anticipation:

> On my way, with pizza rolls in my
> possession. A selection of Hawaiian or
> supreme

> Great. My parents are here so don't worry .
> U will enjoy my mum

I smiled, thinking back to the story from my previous visit.

> Did she bring more magic mints?

> Yes , wait for it !!!!

This should be an entertaining session.

When I arrived, Bails' parents, Bev and Ted, were there before me, tending to their boy as if he were fourteen and home from school with a cold. If there was an audition for an Australian version of the parents from *Everybody Loves Raymond*, then Bails' parents would win hands down, with one exception: in place of the bitterness the Hollywood couple was famous for, Bev and Ted shared a loving acceptance. In their 80s now, Bev was effusive, doting, bubbly; Ted was calm, accepting, gentle. Sugar and, well, more sugar.

And though it was clear Bails was loving the attention, he still hammed it up for visitors. He shot me a long-suffering look as I pushed into the room with a paper bag in each hand.

"As requested, sir." I shook the bags. "Pizza rolls. Times two: choose between ham and pineapple, or supreme."

"Oh, stop it," Bails laughed, a hungry gleam in his eyes. "You can put them over here." He cleared a space on the tray table beside his bed. "This will fit just right, see? I'm starting to work out how to plan my food while I'm here. They give me lunch, but I'm also getting supplies smuggled in at various times. So I need to space out my bread and my fruit."

Bev chuckled as she packed up the morning's paper, stuffing it into a plastic bag to take with them when they left.

"Okay. That's dessert?" I asked, gesturing to a tub of fruit.

He nodded his agreement. "Fruit salad for dessert. But you— you've outdone yourself. You do tend to... You're always thinking outside the square a little bit." Coming from a guy renowned for thinking different, I was quite chuffed.

"I've got people sort of bringing in certain things," Bails continued. "I can't think of anything that Nick Poulos could bring in though."

"Maybe he can be your Sorbolene supplier?" I joked. "You've both got follicle-free scalps to look after. And I now know how much work it takes!"

I ran my hand over my now shaved head, and it still felt foreign. Sando had suggested we all shave our heads in a sign of solidarity for Bails, and everyone on the coaching panel had loved the idea. Bails had loved it too when we sent the pictures through.

I had stopped halfway through the shave, with the sides still on and the top all gone, in homage to the bald head Bails sported au naturale.

75

> They call this look 'The Bailey' ... we r with
> ya all the way mate

> Nice I like the look

Bails had replied deadpan via text that day, and he laughed when we first spoke in person about it.

"That's true," he said with a raspy chuckle, mirroring me by running one hand over his bald head. "He could bring Sorbolene; I never thought of that. Mum's going through it like it's going out of fashion, massaging my feet and all." He wiggled his toes beneath the sheet. "Good on 'ya, mum," he told her, and Bev beamed with pride.

"Or," I began, struck by a thought, "have you ever had those Greek desserts, Profiteroles?"

Bails' eyes lit up. "Or Baklava!"

"I'm sure he could produce something like that."

"Just something he can drop in on the way, just to sweeten the day."

Seeing him at that moment, it struck me how much the simple pleasures from friends can lift a person's spirits. Just the thought of sweets gave Bails a sparkle in the eye.

"Coffee, maybe?" I asked. "Can you have coffee at the moment?"

He shook his head. "I've tried to steer away from coffee and tea at the moment, to be honest."

This was huge news – Bails loved his coffee, and was second only in the caffeine consumption standings to yours truly.

"I can drink it. The doctor said, '*You could have it, just don't go overboard.*' It's like anything else, just eat well. If you like butter, then eat butter – but don't eat ten kilos of it. You just need to try and get the weight up."

He paused, looking troubled.

76

"There's gotta be something else," he murmured, looking down now. A serious face from Bails. "'Cos I can't spell Baklava."

We all laughed at that, the laughter fading as Bails hoed into his pizza roll. The jokes flew back and forth, and at least for that moment, it was almost as though everything was normal: just friends and family spending a bit of time together.

"Hold on, mate." He held up a finger mid-banter, turning toward Bev. "Mum, can you get that wet towel and just wipe this stuff off my feet a bit there? Good on ya', love." Bev ran water in the sink to soak the towel before wringing it out again. "She loves it. Mum loves it." I didn't know about that, but it was clear she loved taking care of her boy, so she put up with it.

"Were you a nurse, Bev?" I asked, impressed by her efficiency.

"No way," she replied.

"But you did raise how many kids?"

"Just two."

"Oh. Okay." For some reason I had expected more.

"We just made the same sort," she told me.

"I thought you always said three?" Ted laughed as he said that.

"Ey?" Bev looked at him like he was out of his mind.

"I thought you would've added me maybe." We all chuckled.

"No," she said slowly, "would've loved a daughter." She looked over at me. "But silly bloke here," she waved a hand at him "could only produce ones with doodles."

"Sounds like all my brothers – eight nephews and only one niece. They just keep pumping out boys."

"Yeah, well Todd's the only one that's produced a girl." She smiled.

"Todd's more girly than me," Bails chimed in. "He used to whine that I had the easiest life ever when I'd call him from work."

Bev ignored his wisecrack, her fingers digging into the balls of his feet. "How's that, love?"

Bails didn't answer right away, savoring her efforts.

"Yeah, you can have a rest now," Bails dismissed her help a few moments later.

For a couple of minutes, we fell silent again as Bev took the towel off the bed. She turned her doting hands to tidying things up around the patient.

"Paddy's looking after High Performance," Bails told his parents, knocking the silence out of the room.

"Yeah," Ted said, "that's good. Would never have been looking after me, then!"

"Nup." Bails picked up his pizza roll again and took a large bite. "So the coaching conference - it went over a day and a half, didn't it?"

I nodded, having just come from a session to visit him today. "They'd just be finishing now, I'd say."

"Ah, right. That's why Doc and Rob Harding are coming in this afternoon." He reached for his cup of water to wash down the pizza roll. "Yeah, I never know about these conferences. People get up, and they say stuff, and you walk out, and you go 'not sure whether I'm a better coach walking out than what I was walking in.' You always get the feeling everyone's hiding everything. Their IP is too precious or they're not prepared to share a few things, because all of a sudden then my tricks are gone, you know. After that I'm no good."

Eyes down, he smoothed the sheet needlessly while he picked through what he wanted to say, and I took the time to tuck into my own pizza roll.

"Geez, you have vacuumed that up!" I'd only made my way through a quarter of the other roll I'd brought.

Bails grunted in agreement while he finished the last morsels. "Yeah. I haven't been too bad on the tooth for the last two or three days."

"There's still a fair chunk of the supreme left here, too," I offered.

"Oh, I know, that's why I wolfed the Hawaiian down, to get to the supreme."

His mum laughed. "He's eaten more than me today!"

His phone went off with a message and Bails picked it up, looked at it quizzically, and then went off to reply. "'Scuse me."

I turned to his parents while Bails taps away a reply. "He takes after you in the appetite stakes, Ted?"

"Um, yeah, I think so. We trained 'em pretty good," he told me, referring to both of their kids. "We used to have a fresh fridge load of food every day when they were growing up."

A gasping, uncomfortable sound swung the attention quickly back to Bails as he began to dry retch. Reaching for the sick bag, he let out a wet burp. It was a false alarm, as nothing else came out.

"You okay, love?" Bev asked. "In here?" She tapped her chest.

"Yeah." Another cough, dry this time, confirmed he was clear. The level of his illness was becoming more apparent though, even from the first visit to now.

He took a bite from the second pizza roll, and his eyes rolled back in pleasure. "Oh..." he moaned, savouring the taste. A rare pleasure for him in this room. "Should've had that one," he said blissfully. "The pizza taste... it's spot on."

"Yeah," Bev said to me, getting back to her favourite topic, "our house always had lots of people there. Didn't we, Dean?"

"Mmmmph," he said, still scoffing pizza rolls.

"One time," Bev continued, "we even had school teachers there! Couldn't believe it. Dunno how they found out about it in the first place. We had a pool table, so it was pretty popular, but one time we had the school teachers come. Now who'd invite your school teachers? I dunno how."

"Well, I didn't invite 'em," Bails said. "You must've invited 'em without knowing and forgot about it. 'Come around next week, or next year.' Then forgot." He turned back to me. "So anyways, where'd we go?

"Just the coaching conference," I offered a starting point. Bails downed the rest of his water and sat silent, neither of us having much more to say on the topic. The pause allowed me to redirect the conversation back to the subject at hand: Bails.

"How bout you mate – how are things in here?"

"Had Triggy just drop in this morning," he replied. As Adelaide's CEO, Steven Trigg was a relationship- based manager, so it was no surprise that he had visited. He also shared an inglorious experience in common with Bails: both of them suspended by the league in the past year.

"Popped in for about an hour, I think it might have been. Was quite good; we chatted about a lot of things. He was good."

Reaching for the half-full bottle of water on the bedside table, he refilled his plastic cup. Only a trained eye could notice the slight change in the movement of his ribcage, favoring the side of the tumor more than he had before. He paused to take another bite of pizza roll and wash it down with a bit more water, then continued.

"Yeah, he was good," he said, picking up the thread again. "Mellowed a little, I think, Triggy. I just – dunno the right word, but – I said to him, 'I feel like moving to Adelaide Oval means more than just a stadium. I don't wanna' pinch the Barcelona 'more than a club,' but I've just got a feeling about Adelaide Oval, as a symbol, what it stands for and what it means to Adelaide as a community. It seems to be there's a little bit of pride back in the place. A bit more confidence."

"Yeah," I agreed, having noted the same thing myself only a day ago. For a moment my mind drifted back to one of our earliest morning conversations. "It's funny what can give people a shot of confidence."

80

Bails had startled me the first morning I walked down the stairs to find him at his computer. In most shared households I'd been a part of through my 33 years to that point, I was almost without exception the earliest riser. Not only that, but the sight of him huddled in darkness over the computer in just his bedwear – grey t-shirt and old boxers – was kind of odd. Even when I did see that he was just cutting edits from last season's games.

"Got a pretty interesting book for my latest read, Paddy." He grabbed my attention, then followed through with a movie-preview voice-over: "*Confidence.*"

"Oh yeah," I laughed at his theatrics, and recalled the big black book with the bold title. "I saw that one on the table. Any good?"

"Not bad – just skimmed it so far to be honest."

"What they say?"

"'*The goal of winning is not losing two times in a row*'" Bails quoted. "All based on psychology principles. Says that as coaches we just need to help them stay on task after bad events, and think laterally to try and solve the problems themselves."

"Interesting. What if they aren't good enough and they do lose twice in a row?"

"Hmm." Bails grunted. "I know what that's like," he said with more than a hint of irony. The silence that followed was an invite for me to explain, and so I did.

"There's a bit of a new school of thought," I kept it rolling, "where some experts say it isn't just about working harder."

"Like who?" Bails probed, ever curious.

"This Stanford professor named McGonigal," I offered one example. "Her work on focus shows that your ability to concentrate on tough tasks improves with support and care from fellow group members, not scolding and shame."

"So theoretically players would be more able to stick at things?" Bails queried. It was his last game as head coach that gave life to the research in Bails' mind. I was momentarily oblivious, and kept on going.

"The science gurus call it 'Ego Depletion'," I explained, "when the brain's batteries wear out from working too hard to control emotions or thoughts. Then it gives in to temptation easier than it might normally do."

"Sounds like what happened in the end to the players at Melbourne," Bails offered. Unsure how open he would be, I left it to him to expand if he wanted to. "Too much going on for them off the field for them to think about what they needed to - especially in that last week before the Geelong game. They just looked like they couldn't do it anymore."

It was a hint of what was to come in my time with Bails - an open book, genuine, without anything to hide.

"Imagine if we were able to train it," Bails daydreamed.

"Well, there's actually a few people who suggest you can," I offered, matter-of-factly.

"Really Paddy?" Bails raised his eyebrows, and the corners of his mouth followed with a mischievous grin.

"I mean, it's just simple stuff that works with school kids at this stage, but..." I hesitated, beginning to question how certain I had sounded.

"You know," he carried on, still grinning, "if we can figure out how to do that with all our guys - that's gold right there."

And just like that, over breakfast, he had planted a seed without me even noticing it.

Back in the room, Bails was busy talking about his own community.

"Of course I had my mates over, and they talk shit for an hour and a half and they left, went back to Melbourne. Drank a few bottles of my best champagne."

I chuckled. "What else are mates for?"

"I said you may as well – not as if I'm gonna miss it!"

For the first time, Bail had hinted at the inevitability of this battle. It was subtle, but it stuck in my mind. Bails went on as if he hadn't acknowledged anything.

"So they had a try, said it was quite good. They went to Ming's... Bing's..." He struggled to remember. "Bing's restaurant, couldn't get in anywhere else."

"Ding Hau?" I supplied, guessing it was the dumpling mecca in town that the more discerning players raved about. I was pretty sure that was the place he meant.

"Bing wow wing, yep – that little place with the Asian stuff. Dingy's. Ah, what else?"

"What else?" I responded to his question with a question to buy some time, still thinking about his little slip before. I was also eager to let him lead the way for now.

"You want a chewy?" Bails asked, and we looked at each other with a wry grin. It was an old joke between us, and I glanced at Bev to see if she was in on it.

"Yeah," she told me, "we've got packets and packets and packets of them." Bails hadn't told her about it, and he didn't fill her in now.

"You can have a choice – soothers, mentos, Juicy Fruit." There was a mischievous gleam in his eyes.

"I'll grab a couple of Juicy Fruit. Like game day."

"You want a whole packet?" Bev called out.

"Nah, I'll be fine with just a couple, thanks, Bev." I paused, then had second thoughts. "My coffee breath isn't that bad, is it?"

"Nah," she shook her head, still insisting I take a full packet. "Here, take it."

"Okay, Bev, I'm not gonna argue with you more than once!"

For the next little bit, it was quiet as Bev made sure I had my choice of chewy. The only sounds were the hum of the lights overhead and the rustle of plastic and paper wrappers.

"I was talking to the doctor today," Bails began, "and he..." A coughing fit overtook him, more severe than the last. When it was over, he wiped his mouth and picked up where he'd left off.

"It's gotten a bit rough, but they're trying to put me on tablets. I've told everyone this, so if I've told you, just let me know."

"No, I don't think you've told me this. You mean tablets as in chemo tablets? Or what?"

"Nah, nah," he said, shaking his head in denial. "They're trying to get me off this pack here," he pointed to the morphine bag that hung from a stand beside his bed, a tube running from it into his arm. "That way I can take tablets rather than having this infusion, which means I'd be better off."

He looked at me to make sure I was following, then pressed on. "See, I wake up in the middle of the night, and I'm trying to lick my lips and wet them, to get 'em open. Like I feel like my lips are stuck together, and if I pulled them apart I'd rip the bastards open. The Doc said to me 'just some chewy's fine,' so I said to Mum and Dad 'can you get me some soothers or something to suck on?' Mum goes and buys me fifty-two packets of soothers and a majority share in Wrigley's."

I chuckled. "That's a good deal."

"So, I don't need 'em all, but anyways – nothing like buying in bulk."

Almost the entire time he spoke after mentioning switching from the morphine drip to tablets, he shifted in his seat. Moving his leg here, twitching his back there, all the while looking uncomfortable and wincing if he moved his back or shoulders wrong. Bev took pity on him and came back over to massage his shoulders.

"So who's training well?" he asked. "Wait, here's an easy one – who's not training well? Who's the problem? Any problem children?"

Bails had a gift for picking up the guys that were falling through the cracks. The fringe players, the ones who weren't on fire.

"Well, Crouchy's still not training, full stop. So that'll be a problem for us once we start playing." Brad Crouch was the prized recruit who had arrived at the Crows the same month as Bails and I. He was a young, raw kid from the country, but great things were expected of him eventually. "He's handling it pretty well right now, better than I thought he would."

" Ah, who else? Brodie Martin stepping up?"

"He's starting to turn."

"What's his issues?"

"He's got more going on than just football. He's the sort of kid you were talking about when we went for a walk on Thursday. If we can make a significant change in him – it's not just a football thing."

"I just wish I could be in there to spend some time with him," Bails remarked. "I think if we get him feeling good, he could really break out this year. Sometimes you underestimate just how important it is for a guy just to feel good."

I nodded, frowning slightly and drumming my fingers on the table as I ran through the playing list in my head.

Bails offered some assistance finding the guys to talk about. "Tex was in here before, did I tell you that? Just off his own bat, he bought me the coffee scroll."

Taylor "Tex" Walker is an enigmatic forward who was one of our most loved players, both inside and outside the organisation. Not only packing some freakish talents in a rather imposing frame, he's the center of attention in the boys' world that is the locker room—exuberant, irreverent, extravagant. His public persona as the everyday, simple country guy, as well as the work he had done raising thousands of dollars for children's cancer charity, meant he was as close as you'd get to the all-around leader. He was still raw, but with a natural inclination towards the people side of the game it was little wonder he had gravitated towards Bails.

"What else?" he asked. Looking out the window, for just a moment he seemed barely aware of his visitors - even Bev, who was still kneading his neck and shoulders.

"Um, The Rat. I'm bit worried about the Rat at the moment. Not sure how he's going."

"K," He shot me a concerned look. "I thought things were going okay with the Rat."

The Rat– Rory Atkins on his birth certificate - was a player closer to Bails than almost any. Not for special talent, though he had plenty of that. And not because he was on the outer: he had enough mishaps in the last couple of years to qualify with honours in that class. Rat was close friends with Darcy, and so Bails was almost an uncle figure to him. A second father even, given he was now away from his family at the age of 19. Bails had heard from another coach that things weren't going that well.

"Pre-Christmas he was running well," Bails recalled.

Another nod from me. "But he's a bit run down. I think he went home one time, not sure. I don't know the full story, 'cos I'm not in the Player Development spot anymore. Emma's going well though; more guys are starting to gravitate to her now."

Emma Bahr, a small woman with a big appetite for helping the players off the field, had a no-nonsense attitude that the players really appreciated. In a world where 95 percent of people either worship the ground you walk on or demand excellence of you, it can be refreshing to have someone treat you like a normal guy. More than most coaches, Bails appreciated the role that played in helping his players grow.

"Oh, well that's good – tough role for her, just starting out."

"Yeah," I agreed, having been in her shoes only a year or two ago, "but I think they've had enough guys test her out now and find she's really good. So they start to trust her a bit more."

"Just give that a bit of a rest now, Mum," Bails said over his shoulder, "and Paddy and I can go for a walk. You can have a rest." She smiled and kissed him on the top of the head, stepping away to do something with the plants on the window sill. Bails turned back to me. "Let's go for a walk, Paddy."

"Yep," I said, hopping up out of my chair, "let's go."

Bails scooted to the edge of the bed and lowered his feet to the floor, reaching for his slippers with his toes. "Can't have Mum's hands working all day."

Once we were out in the hallways, he seemed a little more alive, in part because he wasn't sedated by the comfort of his mum's hands, but also because there was more light out here. He fired the first questions for this walk.

"How's the state team going?" Adelaide had finally joined the other teams in the competition in setting up their own reserve side. Instead of the legacy system of farming the players who didn't play in the main side out to various teams in the second tier state competition, we now had our own feeder side. "Is it set up all right?"

"I think so," I hesitated, given I didn't know all the ins and outs. "I think it'll be great for us, but I think there'll be some teething issues. Like there might be top-up players who clearly outperform players we have on our list. "

We had both seen this issue in the Victorian version of the same system, the VFL. "Those are the problems we'll see coming up during the year," I continued. "I think there'll be no questions of top ups adhering to team style and game plan, there'll be no question marks that they're gonna be the best coaching panel in the SANFL. Unit's pumped."

Heath Younie, or "Unit," was himself a former SANFL captain, and qualified teacher, who had worked his way up to now be in charge of guiding the Crows' reserve side. He was another part of the coaching team who loved the development side, and would occasionally join Bails and I in scheming how we could take the latest learning psychology and infuse it into our training.

Bails looked up to the roof as if trying to access a memory.

"When I was in Melbourne," he began, "we had a property guy – Old Ronnie – he'd been doing it for forty years, I reckon. Got paid nothing, but anyways, he was property steward, full time. Good fella. Melbourne pensioned him off, put him in a motor home or something – this 30 grand thing. They did a good thing, 'cos he had not a cracker to his name, Ronnie. Then Ronnie said I'll only teach one person to do the job. And it's him."

Bails mimed a direct point at the wall to emphasize his point, then continued. "He nominated a bloke who was already down at their reserve side. 'I'm not teaching anyone else,' he says. 'Okay, Ron, no worries,' the GM says. So that's how that transition happened."

I wondered for a second where he was going with his story. I needn't have worried – like a masterful speaker, he circled back to emphasize his point perfectly.

"And that's why you gotta treat everyone the same, 'cos you never know who they are." Bails nodded to emphasize the point.

"That guy at the bottom of the tree with no name was me," he offered as Exhibit A, "when I walked in as a development coach at Essendon. It was you when you arrived here in Adelaide. It was Bill Belichick taking a 25-dollar-per-week job as an assistant straight out of college."

I nodded and smiled at the example, pulled from one of the coaching books Bails loved to devour in his little spare time.

"Plus you don't know what someone might be going through when they leave and go home. Are they fighting with their missus? Is their kid in a hospital? Do they have the bank chasing them?"

He coughed, and then sputtered, "Does their dad have cancer?"

His face shows signs of the welling of tears and a tightening of the throat, but he fights it back and regains his composure.

"You gotta assume the best of people if you wanna help them get where they want to go. That's our job. And if you do it well, you'll get where you want to go, and the rest will take care of itself."

We returned to the room just as Ted was walking out, telling us he was going to move the car before he got a ticket. Bails shuffled out of his slippers and back under the sheet on his bed, glancing over at Bev.

"Come on, love, back to work – on my back." He teased, emphasizing the word "back" both times, reveling in the pun. Bev set aside the magazine she was reading and stood.

"I heard him say please," I added, my voice dripping with sarcasm. "Pretty sure I heard it in there." Ted, still standing in the doorway, laughed.

"Please? Please." Bails played to the crowd.

Bev began to knead his shoulders again. "Just up there a bit, love... yeah, just there and a bit to the left. Can you reach that? I feel like I gotta move back a bit, feel like I should be back a bit." He scooted backwards so Bev wouldn't have to reach so far.

"There we go," she said when he was close enough she didn't have to strain to lean in.

"That's it, just that top third, love. Top third, from about... from there." Making sure she was on the right track, Bev traces her hands from his shoulders down to find the right range. "Keep going, keep going.... There." He stopped her just below his shoulder blades. "From there up. All the way up there, that top part of me shoulders." When she hit the spot, he turned his attention back to our chat, but looked ahead to a shared passion: world sports.

"Who's gonna win the Super Bowl? Once they get the snow off the ground, that is!"

"They're taking a big punt, aren't they?"

"'Scuse the pun!" I laughed.

"Ha ha, good." Bails loved his puns. "I know this is why they don't wanna do it there, they've tried to resist it. One thing that's gonna happen – that coach is gonna be cold!" A highlight of Beckham bending a kick appeared on the television screen in the corner, drawing Bails' attention. The sound was off, no closed captioning, so I couldn't tell what was happening. The announcement of his retirement maybe? "David Beckham. That's brilliant!"

Still working Bails' back, Bev asks, "Is that the spot, love?"

"Yeah," he told her, "that's good, too, Mum. So good you can do it all over my back, that'd be great." He winked at me, before a huge cough exploded from him all of a sudden.

"For some reason, Paddy, I just think," another cough rattling in his chest and throat, "I think Peyton Manning... I think the story is just there. You're always looking for the story behind the big games. It's the story that stands out and grabs the human mind."

"Well," I said, "Funny you mention it, 'cos you'll like the story of the Seahawks. This is one of the things I picked up from them while I was there a few months ago, which we haven't discussed 'cos we got straight back into it. But they pride themselves on their ability to build a team, and the way they look after their players. They've got more guys signed off waivers and undrafted free agents than any other team. They do a lot of their recruiting based on character and profiling, as opposed to what they've done in their college career."

His eyes lit with interest. "Yeah, I didn't know that."

I nodded. "They could be the story of a change in the old way of doing things. And their head coach Pete Carroll is a big believer in psychology and positivity himself. They've infused psychology into their entire program, and their coaches are almost over the top positive. They do things a little different there."

"I like that story. I'd prefer that sort of a story to come out of it than an individual hero – Peyton Manning – which is what the Super Bowl is normally all about."

"They got a sixth rounder and an undrafted free agent, and now they're both pro bowlers. All because they saw – a bit like Nobes does – the ideal profile of a perfect cornerback. He should look like this, he should think like this, but no one likes him 'cos he's played okay, or he's too tall or he's too slow." I took a sip of my own water. "Then they support him, teach him to read the game, so his slowness doesn't matter."

"Nice." He nodded, staring towards the TV, but you could tell he wasn't watching the highlights on the screen. Instead, he focused on a vision in his head. "We tried a similar thing in Melbourne. Just blokes who take most of the intercept marks. 'Cos if someone can learn to take drop-off, intercept marks..." He fell silent again, watching the replay of his memories.

"Well," he finally continued, looking back over at me. "That's as far as it went because I didn't have the time to spend looking at every intercept between handling the CEO's manipulative shit. But, if that's the story with the Seahawks, then I'd be happy to have that story."

"I agree with you on the result, though," I said. "Unfortunately I think the Broncos will win."

"Be a cracking game. Just hope the weather's not that bad."

There was a knock at the door, and it opened a crack. Seeing who it was, I told Bails, "Here's a bloke who'll have an opinion!" And with that introduction, Rob Harding walked in bearing an armful of gifts.

Rob had arrived at the Crows at the same time as we both had, albeit based in Melbourne at first. As our pro scout, he had more work in that city otherwise known as the "Home of Football" in Australia. A friendly, inquisitive and whip smart operator, Rob had moved over this pre-season to spend more time with the players, and also his partner Kat, whom he had met at the club.

"There he is!" Bails said with a smile.

"How are 'ya, mate?" Rob asked, beaming a smile while walking over to Bails' bedside to shake his hand.

"Good, mate. How are you?"

"Good, thanks." He released Bails' hand and started looking around for a place to set the gifts he'd brought.

"Can you just put that in there?" Bails asked, waving toward a little cubbyhole beside the bathroom. Harding obliged. "You're a good man."

"No worries," Rob said, pushing aside the bottle of water and a few plastic cups in various states of emptiness.

"This is my mum, Bev," Bails introduced his mother to Rob. "Bev, this is Rob. My dad's just downstairs moving the car, so he doesn't get a ticket. Why don't you have a rest, Mum?"

"Nah," she told him, returning Rob's hello wave and then getting back to kneading at his son's muscles. "I'm okay."

"Nah, have a rest, love. You're gonna be here for another four hours, so best save something in the tank."

We all chuckled at that: it was funny because it was true.

"We're just talking Super Bowl, Rob Harding," I said.

"Oooooh." He grinned in approval at the topic of conversation.

"So who do you like, big fella?" Bails asked.

"Denver," came Rob's enthusiastic reply.

"Yeah, we're a bit the same."

For the next few minutes, the three of us prognosticated about the upcoming game like panelists on ESPN. Bev returned to a seat on the sideline, catching her breath and following the conversation like a rally in the tennis.

"What's happening in the football world, Rob?" Bails asked after a few minutes, changing the subject as I picked up my phone to turn the Dictaphone off. "Gimme something. I'm starved of new info."

Rob was the perfect guy to ask that question, given his encyclopedic knowledge of the AFL. We slip back into standard banter about what teams were training well back in Melbourne, drugs at Essendon, draftees at Adelaide.

All standard stuff for us, and a comfort for Bails.

SCRIMMAGE TWO

EXECUTION

| | | |

186 points.

It was four points shy of the biggest losing margin in the history of the league.

The fact that it was at the hands of one of the greatest Geelong teams ever, on their way to their third AFL Premiership title in a five-year dynasty, meant little to anyone who was witness to the wheels coming off for Melbourne that day. It was a true "tipping point," one which set off a chain of events that would reverberate well into the next few years.

Deep in the bowels of the stadium, in the area where only a chosen few can access, there was silence. The lack of sound spoke ten times louder, and truer, than the manufactured noise that had filled the locker room a little over two hours earlier. The pre-game buzz had been an attempt by the leaders to raise some spirit in a team exhausted from a week of off-field turmoil. The scoreboard suggested their efforts had been wildly unsuccessful. Given the distractions for the leaders themselves right up to the night before the game, their attempt to right the ship with an hour to go before the game was futile.

On the Monday before the game, then captain Brad Green had set things in motion without meaning to. When pressed on how key relationships were going at Melbourne as a special guest of 'On The Couch', the popular football panel show, his reply left plenty to the imagination.

"We've got a bit of stuff going on off-field that we need fixed to get things right at the footy club," was Green's blunt reply.

EXECUTION

All year the Demons had denied outside rumors that the coach had issues with chief executive, Cameron Schwab, and football boss, Chris Connolly. In reality, the club was a mess on the inside. Players had begun to feel that not only was their coach unsupported, but that they themselves had become political pawns for an administration that was more about image than substance.

For the club's vice-president, Don McLardy, who was taking much of the load of leading the club board in place of the ailing president, Jim Stynes, this was a huge wake-up call. The players' misgivings had appeared in an independent consultants' report to the board earlier in the year. But to this point, the board had taken no notice of the rumblings. They were paying full attention now.

The next day, Don attended what would have been a routine meeting at the club between the coach and his leadership group. The conversation quickly turned to Brad's comments, and the rift.

Bails, feeling uneasy and not wanting to compromise the honesty of the discussion, left the room, and the players opened up to Don. Two days later, with only two days to go before the game, Don called Bails to tell him he had called the leadership group to a meeting with Jim at McLardy's house. Bails reminded Don that the team was travelling to Geelong the following day.

"Jim needs to hear this," was apparently his response.

Every one of the team's on-field leaders attended the meeting, putting everything on the table. Meanwhile, Bails, as he had taught so many young footballers to do, focused on what he could control. He continued to coach and prepare the team as best he could, knowing these emotional after-hours talks were draining his best and most influential players.

By the time the team was in their hotel on the Friday night before the game, key people knew that the club had sacked their chief executive. That included some of the players, who were almost relieved it was over. Bails had noticed how worn down the leaders seemed, and was unsure how much of a impact this would have on the team's ability to take on one of the best teams in the league.

96

Sitting alone with his captain, emotionally and mentally spent, less than twenty-four hours later, he had his answer.

Still dressed in his playing gear, Brad looked over at Bails with an apologetic, confused face.

Side by side, slumped on the floor against the wall of lockers in the away rooms, the last to leave the scene of the horrific massacre. They hypothesised about what went wrong, dissecting the game. Did the fact they didn't kick a goal in the first quarter suggest they were too amped up in the pregame? Did the twelve goals they conceded in the second mean the quarter-time huddle does not have enough spark? In Brad's mind, they were problem-solving so they could make amends next week.

A short silence fell between them as they reflected, a silence befitting of the sombre state for their team right now.

"I think I'm cooked." Bails filled the silence with a bomb. "I think, you know..."

Brad looked up at him, half surprised, but more pleading than anything. "Nah it'll be fine mate," he cut him off and waved his hand.

Green half agreed in the back of his mind - it's a win-loss business, after all, and that was literally one of the worst losses ever. But he felt shattered, because more than the thoughts about the football reality, he didn't want it to be right because of what Bails meant to the players. For them, he had the culture right, the playing group was right behind him, and they were moving in the right direction over the long term. They were just a young team that needed time to keep developing, especially when things were unstable off the field.

"We're one game out of contention," Green pleaded with his coach to remain optimistic. "Everyone has these mishaps, and losses. I know it wasn't a great result today, but..."

"Nah, mate," Bails cuts in again, resigned to his fate, "I think I'm cactus."

The next day, that same state of shock hung like the smell of wet football gear at the Bailey house.

"Thirty-something goals," Bails repeated to himself, part amazed, part horrified.

He had been saying it every so often since Caron and the boys arrived home the night before. They had been at Darcy's high school Grand Final, only becoming aware of the score as his team was about to begin celebrations. The post-game press conference on the TV in the background killed the buzz.

Sitting with Caron as evening fell, Bails' mobile vibrated, and he reached to pick it up. The display showed one name: Jimmy.

Swiping his thumb across the screen to accept the call, Bails answered.

"G'day Jim." He braced himself. When President Jim Stynes was calling, it wasn't going to be for a Sunday chat.

"Dean," Jim gets straight to the point, the softness of his Irish accent emphasised by the illness that he was battling, but tempered by the nature of the news he was delivering. "I'm calling to let you know we're not gonna continue on with you." No accent could soften that hit.

Caron watched as Bails listened and saw his anger rise.

"So that's it then, is it?" Bails bit back. "Fuck me."

The call didn't last much longer, and Bails wasn't listening anyway. The indignity of losing your job over the phone, combined with the backflip of the club from the decisions they'd made only days beforehand to remove the "destructive" Schwab, had him furious. Granted, Stynes was battling cancer, but there were seven other billionaire businessmen on the board who didn't have the guts to tell him in person.

"We'd appreciate if you could keep it quiet until tomorrow," Jim finished the call with a team-first request. Bails didn't answer, and hung up.

For the next few months, he would remain quiet, often saying nothing as he grabbed his jacket and went for a walk by himself late at night, through the streets of Essendon in winter. Caron knew he would always come home, but she still worried about his state of mind. The resentment bubbled away under the surface, with no way to let it out, and no path to make it right.

TRAINING

BLOCK TWO

SESSION 4
STRATEGY
WE TALK ABOUT LEADERSHIP & HABITS

I came off the track on a hot day at the start of February to find a couple of messages from Bails.

> Paddy, broncos – wow wee. Sea hawks
> story IS better

And twenty minutes later:

> Story just gets better play by play!

I shot back a reply as soon as I saw the end result. The Seahawks had positively dominated the Broncos, eventually winning their first ever Super Bowl by a massive margin, 43-8.

> Only just off the track now, didn't get to see
> the game – Wow Wee (with capitals)!!

While I texted him, I'm reminded of a whisper I had picked up on the grapevine, and so I check where he is going to be later in the week.

> Heard a rumor ur going home?!?

> Yes mate, home this week.

It seemed like a great sign of progress, a little win for the cause. I arranged to visit later in the week, and got back to work.

"Good collection over here, Bails." I picked up a book from the shelf near his makeshift bed – all dedicated to pop psychology and coaching – and browsed the blurb on the back. Despite being home again for the first time in a month, Bails was sleeping on the lounge in his living room instead of in his own bed.

"Yeah," he said around a series of coughs. "Some good ones. I think I've read most of them, I can't remember anymore. Di Morrissey's not mine," he added with a chuckle.

I smiled, then waggled the book in my hand at him – *Soup*, by Jon Gordon. "Can I borrow this one?"

"Ah..." He squinted a bit to see which one I had. "Yeah. That's one I haven't read, but it's an interesting one. Flicked a few pages, interesting. "

"What's the basic premise?" I asked as I flipped the red cover open.

"Leaders drive culture, culture drives behavior, behavior drives habits, and habits deliver results," Bails summarized. Then, almost as an afterthought, he added one more detail. "And to drive culture as a leader, you have to build relationships so that you can help change habits."

"Hmm," I grunted, "interesting." Interesting indeed, I thought to myself, given the chats we'd had over the years on that very idea.

"How you travelling?" I asked him as I settled into a comfortable armchair and began to leaf through the book.

"Oh, I'm struggling a bit," he admitted and then shrugged. "Just getting used to being home, that's all." His gaze wandered about the room, lighting for a moment on the television, bookcases, chair, window.

He'd been home for a few days now, released from prison only to be confined to the lounge at home. He couldn't lie in bed for drainage reasons, couldn't sit on the lounge or in a chair for long. In a way, he'd exchanged one prison for another.

His answer demanded attention, and I put the book down to dig a little deeper. "Isn't that better?"

I could see it going either way. Good for the comfort and familiarity, but bad for the same reasons. Wanting to do the things he'd always done, yet unable to because of his failing body.

"It's better being home, but um..." He paused to consider it, a slight frown wrinkling his forehead. "You get used to things, you know. I haven't organised myself for sleep well enough."

Another, shorter series of coughs interrupted him. As soon as it was over, he adjusted the oxygen lines in his nostrils and went on as though it hadn't happened.

"Like, I should be trying to have a kip during the day. But you know, my friends were here last week, and they're here again this weekend. That's fine, I'm not going to stop them from coming, but the only time everyone else has got time to come and see me is today or yesterday..." He trailed off as he picked at the edging on the seat cushion, perhaps not wanting to offend given I was one of the regular visitors.

"Pain?" Although he might not be letting on, the difference in him since my last visit was stark. Pale skin had replaced the natural summer color that most coaches had from spending so much time outdoors. Blue shadows hung under his eye like the paint on a gridiron player, offset by the speckled white of his unkempt stubble. I was curious to see if he felt as average as he looked.

He adjusted his position on the couch, as if the question had reminded him of his discomfort.

"Ah, I've got a bit of pain, yeah. I'll pop a few more pills than I want to just to take a little bit of the edge off, but I'm not too bad. Got chemo again on Friday, so..."

"Is that your first for a few weeks now?"

"Yeah, I have it every three weeks. Three-week cycle. Every morning, the first hour of the morning, I'm ordinary."

He checked himself, and decided he needed more emphasis on that last point.

"Fuckin' ordinary. I gotta' try and find a way to maybe stay in bed a bit longer. First hour of the morning is bloody painful, and then 'cos I have a tablet in the morning, I get a bit drowsy, and then I get a bit tired."

He brings his eyes back to me now, and his words come back to my original question with them.

"Feels better being at home, but doesn't feel better being at home. Dunno how that works. In hospital, you've got the bed at the right height. Here you have to roll out, lift up. It's like a gymnastics routine."

"Hmm," I searched for a summary. "Spiritually better to be at home, but physically not as good?"

"Yeah, yeah, that's it." He shuffled and punched the pillow he had perched himself on, trying to get comfortable at a strange angle. I looked back at his books, looking for inspiration or a good hook to throw out the first question, but Bails beat me to it.

"I was talking to D-Mac about his habits," he touches on one of the topics in the book. D-Mac, known to his parents as David Mackay, was the typical mid-tier player to this point—studious, good trainer, able to fill a role. And yet, before this season, there had only been brief glimpses of his elite potential, short periods of steady followed by weeks of inconsistent or average play.

"It might just be giving him a challenge, to drive in a different way some days, most days, do something different, making a different meal. You just wonder how it's going. You think to yourself, I don't know if it stuck. When you wanna see

how it's going, and you turn around and you ask him, he goes,
"Oh yeah, I feel like I'm getting more touches at training, more
handball receives. I'm looking to be more creative, it's front of
mind to be more creative, and then you see it, and you go...
That's a pleasurable thing you know? It's the best part of
coaching – watching and helping players grow."

He paused, for effect.

"On and off the field."

The way he delivered the final sentence made it clear this
wasn't an afterthought. For Bails, this was where the gold was.

"He's definitely in better form at the moment than I've ever
seen him." My observation seems to go unnoticed – Bails is in the
zone right now.

"That's when you feel like you're having an impact on his
life, let alone football you know? 'Cos that transcends everything
else. His friendships, his relationship at home. Is he married or
not?"

I laugh, already knowing what he is thinking, "Nah, but he
will be soon – she's a ripper."

"He will be yeah; she's a cracker. Very, very smart—Caron
even said she's a captain's wife. She's a leadership wife 'cos
she's..."

He trails off here, perhaps for the first time mindful of the
Dictaphone app that may incriminate him when he's gone. Like a
skilled navigator of tricky interviews, he renegotiates the terrain
by imposing his own story on proceedings.

"See, we had them all round for dinner at my joint, 'cos we
wanted all the girlfriends to come at once. I don't think you get
real true roots in Adelaide without including the girlfriends. So
this year, Caron and I thought we'd invite everyone, all my boys
and all their girls, everyone can come. And the girlfriends who
don't come, we'll invite them back with their guy, and we can
invite 'em back in pairs. And that's when the players will actually
start to get to know each other. My experience is they don't know

each other that well as people – they don't know what they do, or their girlfriends' name."

His enthusiasm seemed to take over at this point, like a crowd on the verge of storming the field after an amazing performance. The thought of going above and beyond what you need to do as a coach to build great relationships between others seemed to light a fire in Bails, igniting a passion that I rarely saw from him during day-to-day meetings.

"But that all takes time," I chime in, barely adding to his point. I didn't really have anything to say – it all rang true to me. "Reminds me of a quote I saw the other day: *If you chop enough wood, the fire will burn when it's time.*"

"Yeah," Bails nods, appreciating the analogy. "That's a good habit for leaders. If we make that better from a small social group point of view… it's just another reason to have a coach with good relationships. But I miss all that."

He needn't have said it – it was written all over his face.

"How you going with all the work?" He looked at me, almost apologetically. "Extra workload..."

"Ah, it's not, not too bad," I told him; it was true enough. "I'm not doing too much more. The only thing I've fallen a bit behind in is tracking how each of the coaches is going with their players, and building that database we spoke about. I know it's happening, but from a bigger picture it's hard to track the progress without enough time."

"Hm. How's the coach development going?"

"Good. We had the best session we've had so far last week. Got the guys started talking about their own performance on game day: 'How's my performance as a coach?'"

Bails raised his eyebrows. I leaned forward, resting my elbows on my knees. I knew he would be into this.

"So we just scribbled down some ideas," I continued. "What does a high performing coach look like? What do you deliver? Did you prepare well? How do you review yourself? How do

105

you review each other? I think as long as we standardize it, and refer to it often, I think ..."

"Like a marking sheet or something," he cut in, nodding slowly.

"Yeah – just something so that the coaches don't just come in and go 'geez, the players were shit'," I elaborated, "or 'shit, how good are these players.' Maybe as coaches we can look at it and say 'you know, we could've communicated a bit better here.'"

Despite his lack of energy thanks to the treatment, it was clear this idea had Bails enthused. It was similar to something he had suggested last pre-season, but his suspension had come before he could put it in place. He nodded and his furrowed brow lifted, looking like a contented Obi-Wan Kenobi as he saw his young student grasp an important concept.

"I've thought a lot about that since my time out last year," Bails confided, "just listening to the gameday audio in the box. As coaches, we all know the power of habits: when a player is so predictable 'cos he turns to one side under pressure. Or he lays off his kick when there's none. We bitch and moan about him. We spend hours trying to fix the 'errors'."

I laughed here, knowing full well the examples he had in mind from the last couple of years.

"It was that book you gave us with the Tony Dungy part," he continued, "*The Power of Habit*, that really got me curious about how we could do it better."

The book he was referring to, by Charles Duhigg, was one of Bails' favourites. Duhigg had pulled together strands of research from all over the different sciences and tied them nicely to stories about real world examples like Tony Dungy, head coach of the Indianapolis Colts in the NFL. The end result was a great book with a basic model that has proven effective across a whole bunch of fields. From drug addiction to overeating, to exercise, to relationships, it had worked miracles for people with the most hard-wired behaviours.

"So we know that it works," Bails continued, "but we barely touch it for ourselves, do we? You spend hours preparing the tactics for the game. Another hour crafting your pre-game address, and an extra 30 minutes making contingency plans in case Plan A doesn't work. But what about the stuff you know comes out under pressure?"

"Yep," I agreed, "that can derail your tactics or undo a great speech in a heartbeat."

"How did it work again?"

"Identify the cue, keep the same reward, and just substitute a new routine in between," I recited.

"That's it," Bails paused for a cough, and then nodded. "Its like a recipe for anything in life you want to change. So for us, what's the coach's cue? What do they do when X happens?"

He looked over at the window, and for a moment I could see a wistful look, as if he was wishing he could go and stand there by that window. Without having to adjust his nose tubes. Without worrying about drainage. Wishing to just be normal and look out at the blue sky and clean sand of the beach.

"But those habits don't just change overnight, whether it's a coach or a leader or any other player," he went on, focusing on the distraction instead of his current prison cell. "It takes time. Plus you have to prioritize the right things to make habitual, so they become your default."

I let the silence hang. Bails had hit the nail on the head about something which actually set him apart: his ability to infect guys – players, leaders and even other coaches – with a team-first attitude just through his own example.

"It's a balancing act," Bails said as he balanced his coffee while driving us to training one fresh summer morning. "It's hard to be the nice guy as a leader and still win."

I saw a chance to surprise him. "You know the latest line suggests that 'soft' touch can make you even tougher to beat." Bails raised his eyebrows and pretended to choke on his coffee.

We had begun comparing who we had each worked with prior to landing at Adelaide, before talking about the pros and cons of different coaching styles as a spin-off. "Is that so?" he probed after he was finished with his mouthful of mocha.

"According to a guy named Adam Grant, it is." Before he could ask, I gave him the detail. "He's an organisational psychologist at the best business school in the world. He had the inkling when he was a student that those who cared about others produced better results, so he set about conducting a stack of studies on the topic."

With the encouragement of Bails, I went on to feed him a short summary of the latest on my reading list at the time, Grant's bestselling '*Give and Take*'. Bails nodded along as I outlined the three main strategies people employ when it comes to dealing with others: people take as much as they can with no regard for others (Takers), give as much as they can with no regard for themselves (Givers), or attempt to find a balance between the two by playing tit-for-tat (Matchers).

"And the loser is?" Bails asked, with tongue in cheek.

"Well," I chuckled, "across all the studies, the Givers lose. It seems they are easier to trample on, take advantage of, and generally leave themselves open to exploitation."

"So the winner must be..." he egged me on, curious where it was headed.

"Funny thing is, it's neither the Takers or the Matchers. The Givers dominate the top of the charts just as much as they dominate the bottom."

"How's that work?" Bails was sceptical.

"Turns out that it's more about the *way* you give, rather than *whether* you give, that determines if you climb the ladder or get trampled on. When people are what he terms '*otherish*' —

giving in ways that will benefit them too — they win. And this *'otherish'* behavior also shows up as a factor in improving team results"

Bails eyebrows lifted at this point as we rolled to a red light.

"Right after 9/11," I rolled onto the best example that stuck in my mind, "a group of Harvard psychologists looked into US intelligence agency teams to determine their effectiveness. They found that the strongest predictor of performance was the amount of help they gave to each other. Leaders of highly effective teams helped one another, openly collaborated and shared information. The lower rated analyst groups worked in isolation, barely helping each other."

Bails nodded with his eyebrows even higher now. I could see it resonates with him, and it was obvious why – we'd already discussed plenty of times how he preferred his leaders: direct and genuine, with a low tolerance for bullshit.

"You gotta have a mix," Bails tied the conversation back to the original topic of the drive - picking our first leadership group at Adelaide - as we turned into the staff parking area. "Good players, hard guys, but also guys that care. But your job as their coach is to teach them *all* the same thing - to let go of themselves and give into the team when it's time."

Back in his living room, Bails had paused at the same time as my thoughts drifted, and he was now silently scratching at a spot on his arm. Another coughing attack took him, and when it let go he reached for a nearby bottle of water and sucked down a decent gulp.

"Maybe that's why I'm..." He took another quick pull of his water bottle and then set it down. "I've had a lot of time to think about a lot of things – maybe I've got too much time to think. But maybe that's the point that I keep coming back to, the fact that our blokes are still gonna mature a bit more. It takes time. And I think they'll find that if they mature a bit more, they might get the best out of themselves as well."

And there it was: the other reason why Bails was so strong on developing the young man within the footballer: not only does it help prepare the kid for the rest of his life. It helps the kid become a winner at the same time.

"Sando spoke to me about the leaders on Thursday," Bails pivoted, turning to a topic he had always loved to debate – over the watercooler, a coffee or a good red wine. I hoped his passion for the people side of the game would take over, even if the setting were a little more sterile than the backdrop to our previous chats on leadership. "How were they voted in again?"

I chewed through what seemed like a labourious explanation, going to great lengths to avoid any leadership jargon or buzzwords. I wasn't a fan of them at the best of times, but Bails was especially skeptical.

"Basically, the guys we have are the ones who have the trust of the players we can trust," I summed it up as succinctly as I could. "And in the end, we were surprised by how strongly the guys said, 'Nah the skipper's still gotta be VB.'"

VB, full name Nathan Van Berlo, was Adelaide's incumbent Captain. A surprise elevation to the role for the 2011 season based on his no-nonsense approach to being a professional, he had since won most critics over. Only a week before the announcement, however, a freak accident had cut him down in his prime – a weighted sled had come loose and severed his Achilles tendon. He wouldn't play again this season, making the leadership group an even more important decision this year.

"That doesn't surprise me."

"Why not?" I inquire, keen to hear his view on such an important topic.

110

"Oh," Bails paused and looked up at the roof as if the words he was looking for were hanging from the curtain rails next to his makeshift bed. "They need stability. Especially Tex."

"And big Tex is in!" I exclaimed, knowing he was one of the players who had spent more time than most under Bails' tutelage since we arrived in 2011.

"That's good," Bails nods, but then pauses. "Just a couple of occasions. He's been round to my joint a couple of times..."

His voice trailed off as if troubled by what he has observed but unable to find the words – or perhaps unsure of whether he should – to describe what he had felt.

Bails nodded again. "Tex is a smart dude, but sometimes he can be a little bit over the top." He chuckled as he recalls a private memory, possibly a prank that big Tex was synonymous with. "There's good supporting cast members there now though. Different backgrounds, different strengths, links with certain groups of players."

I smiled inside, almost chuffed that he recognized the deliberate design of the group. "I think the group now is much more representative of the whole team. Those players who have different strengths get different jobs. And with Tex – he wasn't sure, was a bit reticent at first. But he came to me the day VB went down and said, 'Looks like I don't have any choice now.'"

"He read the play," Bails said with a satisfied air. It reminded me of Mr. Miyagi watching Daniel-san master his first move in Karate Kid. "Yeah. That's good. It's a bad situation, and the fact that he says, 'Okay, I gotta help my teammates out here.' He's giving himself to the team."

I nodded, equally as proud of the player I'd seen grow the most as a leader since we arrived two years earlier. "That's a hook that's his. The psychology of it is the key."

"Yeah." Bails agrees, and continues with an example using the nickname of the biggest star on our team. "I think about Danger." Patrick Dangerfield was the media darling of our team, the 'sexiest' of the players from a PR and marketing perspective. Even his nickname had charisma. Well-spoken, well-raised, and still a flashy player with speed to burn—and an insatiable, competitive attitude. Media boffins had anointed him as the future captain perhaps even before our arrival. When all they saw was the natural talent that overflowed from this precocious athletic specimen on the field, not everyone was familiar with his considerable upside thanks to plenty of room for growth as a leader.

"Danger's got a massive part to play with that maturing and leading side. You can't put too much pressure on because he'll divert his attention to that. Sloaney's good too, but it's almost like they still need a couple of wise heads to be around him. Guiding him. I don't think he's someone that all of a sudden it's just going to—" Bails made a sharp click with a snap of his fingers, then continued, "dawn on him and he'll be amazing. It grows, like any other skill."

"Well, if you look at it from a pure leadership psychology point of view," I offered a complementary example, "a leader needs to act on behalf of the group, right?"

"Yeah," Bails confirmed, and then summed up my point for me. "It's great if the leader is a star performer. But it's even more powerful if their default is all team, and zero about themselves. And that's just another habit that you build, over time."

"Who's the best leader you've seen in football?" I ask, sensing an opportunity to draw on Bails decades of experience at the top of the game.

Bails didn't hesitate, "Terry Daniher was pretty good. Timmy Watson wasn't bad, but it was Terry for me."

I had met Terry - or TD, as everyone in the football world knew him - when I was struggling to stay in the league. Cut from Richmond, I went to try out with Essendon two summers in a row, and TD was the coach who handled us during the tryouts. Salt of the earth, personable, but willing to work as hard as we were despite his already legendary status, I could immediately see what Bails was seeing.

"Terry led because he trained harder than anyone," Bails expanded on his answer, "and he performed, and he led by example on the track. He wasn't a great talker, he was pretty straight up and down, was TD. You just had great confidence in him 'cos you knew that he's gonna run himself into the ground. And the guy who was playing on him just knew they were never gonna stay with him. So did he, and he thrived on it."

"Using TD as an example," I bring the focus back to the topic at hand, "I suspect part of his power as a leader came from how authentic he was. Nothing was fake, TD was just TD: 'I'll go balls out on the track, give you everything on game day, and go sink five beers with you after. Not gonna pretend anything'."

"That's exactly what he was like." Bails smiled at this.

"Tex is a little like that," I observed, looking for his response.

Bails started, and then re-worded. "I don't think Tex is angling himself for the main role."

"Nah," I confirmed, "I asked him actually. We had a coffee, and he was showing a lot of interest in who we were going to make leaders. I wanted him in the leadership group, for the balance, and to stretch him a bit. He even helped set up that camp to talk about leadership. And so I said to him after the camp: 'I'm just gonna put it on the table here... Do you wanna be captain of this team?'"

"And what did he say?" Bails was intensely curious about this little story.

"'Nah, shit no!' were his exact words," I tried my best Tex impersonation. "Would never want to be captain. 'I just want what's best for the group,' he says."

Bails either doesn't like my impersonation, or doesn't notice it. "Why doesn't he wanna be captain?"

113

"I reckon he'd feel..." I searched for the right words. "He's a man of the people, and maybe he thinks you can't be one of the boys if you're captain."

"Yeah, you're exactly right," Bails chuckled. "That fits him perfectly. Every now and again, he'll have a view on some things, but I still need my boy time."

"And that might change again in two years," I said offhand. "He might find a girl, settle down..."

Bails picked up the musical thread. "If he wants to, he can marry." No tune to his voice, but I was happy to still hear his humor, as dry as ever.

I took the lighter moment to mean he was feeling okay about going a little deeper.

"I know last time I visited you in hospital," I began, "I thought you seemed better in spirits, and you said you thought it was a result of a longer break between treatments. You were just starting to come up for air a bit. Are you still trending up like that? Or tracking like you were last time?"

"Oh, I've been home for three days now. And every day I'm home, I think I'm feeling a little bit better. To be honest, Paddy..." he paused again, fiddling with his oxygen tube. At first glance he was just adjusting his air. His next words suggested he might have been buying some time to hold his emotions down.

"I just need the chemo to give me a couple of little wins. The radiation's given me a couple of little ones, but just small ones. The lump is getting a little bit smaller. The oncologist says there are some encouraging signs." He rolled his eyes, the picture of skepticism, and shot me a wry grin. " Yeah, great. But I need this chemo, this next bout, to just show a little bit of improvement. You know, just a couple of wins to keep me going, I think."

"How do you measure your improvement?"

"They'll take a CT scan and compare, I guess." Bails saw an analogy and rolled it out for my benefit. "Its kinda like any game plan: you have to set something in place, then back it into a degree. There's no magic pill that –" Bails makes another click with a snap of his fingers, "makes you better. You only get somewhere when you keep your nose down at the grindstone, you know. So we keep treating it, and we'll check every now and then how it's going. You gotta have something to measure every now and then. Just not every day."

His mind returned to the cancer. "But I know that it's spreading. Without trying to measure, I can feel it every day. Spreading through here." He lifted both hands, one to raise his left arm, the other to draw a large swathe across his left ribcage. "Caron and I both know that. It's like a massive lump of concrete moving through me. I wake up in the morning, and I lie there for half an hour or something. That's why my bed's on this angle."

"For drainage?"

"Yeah, might be a bit of that, but it's on this angle 'cos that's what it was in the hospital. I'll lie like that, and it takes a bit to get moving each morning. But I just need chemo to start working. Radiation's been good, so just hoping I can get a little bit better and the hot weather can piss off!"

We both laughed pretty hard at that, but it didn't last as another coughing fit followed.

Once he had cleared his lungs again, he looked up. Exhausted, he began to pull himself up on the couch.

"Well," he wheezed from the effort, "I might need to kick you out."

"No probs," I moved first, not wanting to drain him. "No need to get up."

He was glad for the reprieve and settled back again. I reached for my borrowed book.

"Maybe next time we can sit out on the porch and enjoy the sea breeze!" I try to offer some hope.

He half nods, then offers a tired wave as I close the front door.

Out on the street, the sea breeze was a fresh reminder of how, despite being released from his hospital cell, Bails was still imprisoned upstairs.

I tapped a quick note into my phone, not wanting to lose the little nugget on coaching that grabbed me during today's visit before gazing at the horizon across the water:

There's no magic pill for getting better.

I close my eyes, and find myself wishing the next treatment will give him something to look forward to on the horizon. Bails was a perfect example of today's topic – he just kept giving, a habit that made him a leader guys loved.

If anyone deserved a break, it was Bails.

BREAKFAST WITH BAILS

| | | |

The warm bayside air was so quiet, Bails could hear the gentle waves lapping at the shore about 100 meters from his porch. A high-pitched whine shattered the serenity as two scooters cruised down the esplanade and pulled up in front of the Bailey house.

"What the bloody hell are you doing up there?" Bernie Vince yelled. Despite having played in the AFL for more than seven years now, he still maintained a youthful enthusiasm to match his boyish grin.

"Just taking a breather for a second after whipping up a storm in the kitchen," Bails called back. "Meatloaf. For four," he added, playing along with the script they had perfected after many unannounced visits from the pair. He began counting out the names on his guest list with his fingers: himself, Caron, Mitch, Darcy.

Bernie persisted, knowing full well this ritual would end with them feasting alongside their personable coach. "I reckon there's room at your table for another two, for sure."

His partner in crime, Tex, honked his horn to add an exclamation mark to the suggestion.

Bails doesn't answer, turning back inside to tend to the meal preparations. Caron popped her head out and with a smile and a welcoming line, waved them up to join the family.

Once upstairs, the two footballers settled in to chew the fat with Mitch, Darcy and Caron as Bails put the finishing touches on his "award-winning" meatloaf.

Bernie and Tex were celebrity figures in the fishbowl that is Adelaide city. But sitting at this table they were just a couple of boys

117

from the neighbourhood, their own dry humour right at home in the Bailey household.

Each of the young men at the table took turns poking fun at Bails, two from within his family and two from without. Caron's laughter only encouraged them. He'd spent a good chunk of time making a dinner that he had pumped up as deserving of Masterchef fame. But unfortunately for Bails, the banter had distracted him just enough to ensure the meatloaf had come out on the dry side.

As he took it out of the oven, and attempted to present it as well as he could given its lack of moisture, the laughter began. He carried it to the table with a wry grin on his face, a subtle admission that he might've just missed the mark here. This, of course, was like pouring hot oil on an open flame, and the boys were more than happy to roast him for it.

Bails took it all with a smile, laughing along and giving as good as he got. The similarities with the house he grew up in - a drop in point for all the boys - were striking, and comforting all at once.

And at the head of the table sat Bails, a down-to-earth father figure for more than just his own boys. That's just how the Bailey house worked.

SESSION 5

PATTERNS

WE TALK ABOUT PASSION & PRACTICE

It was surreal to be walking into the hospital again so soon. The quiet noise of the nurses and the plain walls were so familiar, and yet Bails was now in a different room.

He had gone back into hospital when his condition deteriorated only a few days after I had visited him and his makeshift bed in his living room. His dependence was beyond what he and Caron could handle at home now.

My first thought when I heard about the setback was that he could do with some support now more than ever.

> Hey mate, hope you're holding up ok- how would you be if I smuggle you something good for brekky tomorrow?

His reply was fairly business like, understandable given that the business on his plate was literally life and death.

> Paddy , chemo tomorrow in hospital. All morning. But if u drop the stuff off room 440 south ward

Even knowing I wouldn't see him, I decided I would still go through with the ritual the next morning.

> Ok mate- you shall have pizza rolls waiting for lunch then!

119

It was the least I could do, I told myself on the drive down, stopping at the same bakery and grabbing the same order. I even picked up a mocha at the café, for old times sake.

Navigating my way to the new room, I was deep in thought about training that week when I turned the corner.

To my surprise, Bails was sitting right there, perched on the side of the bed, facing the door.

"Paddy!" He wheezed, his enthusiasm for a visitor still evident despite the fatigue. Seemingly breathless from one word now, he waved me in with a tired arm as I hesitated at the door.

"What happened to the morning chemo plan?" I asked as I walked in and wheeled a visitors chair around in front of him so he didn't have to move.

"Postponed it," Bails observed with a wheeze as I sat down. "Gotta make some big decisions in the next couple of hours, I think. The next course of this: radiation, chemo, or tablets."

"You make that decision?" I asked, surprised.

"Mm." His arms were braced against the hospital table next to his bed, and he leaned over it, only just looking up at me. This position was familiar to anyone from the world of contact sports: the instinctive posture you assume after being winded. Fixing the arms allows other muscles to help your diaphragm out as it fights to open the ribcage. It was a sensible strategy for Bails given one lung was almost completely out of action now.

"What guidance do they give you on that? Much info?"

"Side effects, that sort of stuff." He wheezed, his speech even more muted than before, now limited by a swollen tongue to add to his fading lungs. Still he pressed on, "You know, there's a one percent chance of this; that scares the shit out of me. There's a one percent chance of that, and that scares the shit out of me."

The silence hangs, like the hospital gown now draped from his once burly frame, which seemed to be shrinking with each visit now.

120

"But regardless of what I choose, things aren't moving anyways." Wheeze. Cough. Breathe. "My bowels are basically frozen. And my emotions are...."

The chin quivering was the first thing I had noticed, before a deep breath to fight off the wave of feelings welling up inside him. I allowed the silence to hold, giving Bails time to compose himself before I asked the question that might help him find his way through the swell.

"When things set you off, what do you focus on to help?"

"It's little things. Little things set me off," He takes the bait, but swims even deeper with it. "Like, I find myself watching funeral ads. It's surreal, 'cos they never meant anything..." He trailed off as the waves rose again, then composed himself with another raspy breath before continuing.

"I think about my boys," he pines, diving even deeper. "It wasn't that long ago that I was having a kick with them on the MCG, after my first-ever win." He lets out a sob now. "They're just becoming men now, and I can't be there to see it." The tears crash down on his face as the wave overwhelms him this time.

"I wish it weren't like that mate," I offer, placing a hand on his shoulder, which is no longer as strong as it once was. Saying sorry doesn't seem right here – this is no-one's fault, and my pity wouldn't help in any way. "To be honest," I turn to a positive, "I've been amazed at how well you're holding up with that looming in the corner twenty-four seven."

He looks up, wiping the tears away. "When everyone leaves," he is settling now, taking good pauses between each effortful sentence. "When I'm all alone – that's when I'll sit here and cry." Breath. "But it's when people are back." Cough. Breathe. "Then I'll spark up again." Wheeze. Breathe. "Even knowing people are coming helps."

I'm struck by the words he had spoken to me what seemed like ages ago now: people matter. Now, more than ever, that was true for Bails. It seemed like that was almost all he had left to persevere and fight for.

Given the fact he didn't have many positives on that front in the present moment, though, I decided against digging deeper. Instead I took the opportunity to bring the conversation up by shifting to coaching, pivoting away from his emotional struggles like a player avoiding a block.

"Do you think your coaching or playing background might mean you've got a better ability to control emotions and your focus? Compared to someone else who might be going through this?" It was a leading question, but I think both of us were happy to come up for air now.

"Not sure, Paddy," he replied honestly and without hesitation. "It's more the ability to decide in advance how to handle things."

"And does that include deciding what are the right things to focus on?" I tried to keep his focus on keeping focus.

"I guess that's part of what makes a great coach, isn't it?" Bails suggested. "Make the right decisions, at the right time." He had summed it up again. Simple, succinct, and spot on.

"Yep." Nothing more to add here, Your Honour.

"That's always a challenge, every day," he took the theme and ran with it. Slowly. "You've got the football program that comes to you," he breathes, "and everyone asks questions." Lifting his arm to point, he added, "'What about this', 'What about that'."

The extra movement didn't help, and he quickly returns to the brace position. He coughs, and continues. "So you're getting the physios, the doctors, you get the fitness advisors, players..." Breathes and goes again. "You've always got someone who's prepared to give an opinion, or ask, 'What is it you want me to do?'" He takes a sip from the plastic cup on his table. "Plus there's always people challenging what you're doing."

Though it was still hard work for him, his breathing seemed a little easier now than when I arrived. Hard to tell if it was the topic, or the simple act of talking that helped more.

"I didn't mind that so much," he pressed on. "I preferred the discussion rather than the autocratic way." That was no surprise. Bails was a people person at heart. "I'd never be like *'Just shut up and do what I want'*. I could've been a bit harder in that way – 'shut the hell up and do it, this is what we're doing.' Rather than trying to manage my way through situations, I should've just been a lot harder at times."

He sniffed, wiped at his nose, coughed into the crook of his elbow, and then picked up again right where he'd left off.

"And that's a big thing on the people side, with the players - when to be hard, and when not to. Leigh Matthews gave me some good advice."

"Lethal!" I interjected as he paused to breathe. Matthews was a legend in our sport, as both past player and coach. If we handed out rings for every championship you played or coached in like the NFL did, Leigh wouldn't have enough fingers.

"He said to me," Bails continued, "'when the players are up and about, you gotta be the opposite of them'. So that means that when they are down and out, you gotta be providing them with some confidence. And when they're flying, you gotta keep them grounded. You gotta be a bit the opposite of what they are. Um..." He searched for a summary.

"The Yin and Yang," I supplied.

"Mmm." He nodded. "Which I thought was pretty good advice."

"Definitely."

He adjusted himself against the table again, getting restless. "I presume a walk is not on the menu for you anymore?"

"No way I could get round the ward." He looked dejected, and then like a fighter resting between rounds, he lifted his head. "We could try around the bed though."

I smile, and he smiles back. Almost. Slow but steady, I help him out of his chair, taking much more weight than the previous times I'd helped him up.

We shuffle left around the base of the bed, at a much slower pace this time compared to our previous tours of the ward only a week or two ago.

"You notice we turned left again?" I observe, more as a conversation starter than anything. I knew Bails was big on habitual behaviours, and hoped this might start a thread I was keen to explore with him: how to change a young person's habits, the root of their character.

"Must be habit," he joked. His voice was dry, but at least he was picking up what I was putting down.

Toward the end of the previous season, a couple of books we shared had sparked Bails' mind. Most notable were a couple of nuggets about psychology of habits and the tricks to changing them.

"You still brushing your teeth with your left hand?" He looked at me sideways, like a teacher checking on his pupil's adherence to the homework he'd laid out. This was just one of the tricks Bails had latched onto in the book, and he knew we had both picked it up.

"Yep. You still wiping with your left?"

"Ha!" He laughed out loud at this, which prompted a strong cough, and stopped him in his tracks. Once he had his lungs under control again, he looked back up at me.

"Only on Tuesdays," he replied in sarcasm, a little reminder of what we've set out to do with these visits.

Grinning, we reached the other side of the bed, and turned around. On the way back to his sitting spot, he began describing where he had wanted to take the program this pre-season before this had all gotten in the way.

It was a topic we had talked about often – the competitive mindset required to get better at something - albeit in more suitable surroundings than an off white hospital room. Teach a kid to compete and persist at something he loves, even if he isn't great right now, and you can guarantee he'll get better faster.

"Generally," Bails kept on, oblivious to the slight interruption, "if you've been beaten in a final or you played really badly in a game, or you missed a goal, or you know you didn't go hard enough for the ball or something... It's normally sporting scenarios. I've never said that about a math exam. Shit, I should've known M = C squared. Should've nailed that. I've never been dirty on myself for not nailing that. But I've been dirty for missing a goal or whatever."

Voices and rapid footfalls carried up the hallway, and I looked over at the door. As the sounds grew louder, a kid shot past. I heard his dad call for him to slow down, and then a moment later the man hurried past, trying to catch up. Another set of voices started heading our way. I got up to close the door so we could talk with fewer distractions.

"I reckon they're some of the busiest places ever, hospitals," Bails observed.

I laughed at that but then returned to the subject at hand. "Do you reckon that comes 'cos you love football more than you love math? So you want it more."

"Yeah. I couldn't give a shit about school work." He snorted. "Oh, that's not true – PE, I did care. Yeah, sport was more my way out, if you like. When I say my way out, it was what I was good at. Whether it was soccer or cricket or any ball sport; I was pretty good at most things. It seemed that every time I tried something – if it was a sporting thing I had to be good at it. It was my challenge, I guess." This time when someone passed by in the hall, the door muffled their voices.

"So," Bails continued, "when I'd see Sir Donald Bradman hitting a golf ball up against the tin water tank – you know, that famous footage that you saw as a kid – I used to go out the back for hours with a golf ball on a stick, just hitting the golf ball around, tapping it up and down. I used to play tricks all the time. I didn't know what the hell I was doing, but I knew it was challenging.

"I was trying to get to twenty and thirty and forty in a row. That's when the deliberate practice stuff... when I started to read about that, I thought: *'Bloody hell!'* I was doing it without knowing it! And most sports people who get to the elite level... You would've done something similar." He paused, and my mind drifted back to one of our first conversations from our time living together.

Bails had always especially liked the scientific approaches which gave the expectation: if you do *x* consistently enough, you will get *y*. That's why the 10,000-hour rule he first discovered in Daniel Coyle's *Talent Code* appealed to him: train properly at something for 10,000 hours and you will master it. In a small way, that was probably why we hit it off early days.

Not that he needed me to tell him about it. The idea of deliberate practice was something he already knew quite well, from his own experience as well as watching others. Give them a small menial task, make sure they do it properly, and it can shift larger behaviours that may be holding them back.

"I remember setting up a plant in the back yard. We used to have these rafters..." He bought me back to the room, and at the same time he took me to his childhood home, raising a hand up, palm toward the floor. "They're about eight feet above the ground on this pergola running across." He spread his arms out wide. "And I got this potted plant and cut the bottom of it out, only about this big at the bottom," – with both hands, he indicated a circle about fifteen centimeters across – "and I got a little softball that I could throw over the rafter. And if I threw it at the right height, I could put it through. It was like a basketball ring."

He was no longer in the hospital room now; he was back in the yard, ten years old, and loving it.

"I'd just compete with myself, every day, and slowly I'd get a bit better."

Compete, and then repeat, I thought to myself. Bails was oblivious to my mental note – he was rolling now; his body animated as he relived his childhood.

"First it was, *'This is awesome!'* Then I'd make it harder and it was like, *'This is a bit tricky'*. It's like that with players - we have to push them to the point where they go *'this is shit'*.

He was right in the groove now, talking about a topic that clearly got him juiced.

"Like anything you want to be good at in life, you might feel like, *'I'm shit'* at first, but if you can stick with it, soon it becomes *'This might be ok'*. And once you're there, it's all good – you gain mastery over it and start to think it's awesome again – then you also think *'I'm awesome!'* Because you pushed through it."

A quick cough was all that belied his health right now, and he ploughed on with a passion.

"It was that *Talent Code* thing," he began, referencing the book that had generated plenty of conversations between Bails, Unit and I. "The way he described neural pathways. How you can re-route them or make the right ones more ingrained with..."

He paused, though it didn't seem this was to cough, but rather to search for a word.

"Myelination? Plasticity?" I chimed in with the terminology, then expanded in the hope of giving him an extra few seconds to get a decent breath given how staccato his speech was. "Basically you make more synapses and thicker nerves through repeated use of the right pathway, so it eventually becomes the default."

"I was gonna say practice, but yep," Bails continued on, not concerned with the label or big terms. "We can do that. So long as we don't let people slip into bad habits. Practice the right way."

Bails had loved the overlap of both Coyle's book and another, *Outliers* by Malcolm Gladwell. Along with biographies of great coaches, he loved these types of books, which were the perfect vehicle to deliver snippets of psychology wisdom to high-level coaches who didn't have the time, skills or the patience to do the grunt work that is academic research. They had a few critics in the scientific world for being superficial with the research, but at least they opened up the field to the eyes of those who could actually put it to use.

"Like the goalposts," I nodded. "Repeated practice under constraints."

Together we had come up with the idea of shifting the practice field posts in half the distance this pre-season, making a tighter goal to aim at when practicing. I sensed a chance to share some current news on this very theme. "You remember that NBA shooter who had the ridiculous practice routine?"

"Yeah?" Bails sensed the excitement & fresh news.

"Kyle Korver," I supplied the name just in case. "He's currently on the longest streak of consecutive games with a 3 pointer in NBA history."

"Oh boy wowee!" His enthusiasm brought a coughing laugh after he delivered his favourite phrase when trying to play up a sense of excitement, borrowed from one of the most colourful commentators in the game, Brian Taylor. I laughed along, pleased we could summon some good emotion to the room.

"I wonder," Bails posed as he settled, harking back to our initial chat about the poster-child for practice, "how many people think he's doing that based on pure talent?"

"Love the links Paddy," Bails had appeared in the doorway of my office with coffee in hand.

Usually the time it took for him to appear in my door was a direct correlation with how enthused he was by an idea. In this case, I'd only emailed him maybe half an hour earlier with an article about NBA sharpshooter Kyle Korver. The story highlighted his extreme practice habits, along with a facebook link that detailed a grueling preseason training session which would put the best of us to shame: a Misogi, basically an exercise in pain and self-torture.

"He's really packing in his 10,000 hours aint he?" Bails referred to one of his favourite principles.

"He's been doing it since high school apparently – never been highly rated – barely got offers to go to college even – but he just keeps getting better." I dropped a couple of facts re: his pathway to the NBA that weren't in the article.

"I saw this thing on ESPN the other day," Bails picked up the story and raised me. "The World Series of Poker. They showed how the best card players make such great decisions: they know the value of a hand, and what others will do, just from having played so much. They just know."

"That's how the *Blink* concept works," I made the link to another book he loved, "the chunking of experiences thanks to practice. Basically experts can see whole pictures much better thanks to lots of exposure, and the decisions almost make themselves."

We both nodded for a second, on common ground.

"But how do you grow it?" Bails nudged the chat along.

"Well the cool thing is, that grit stuff we talked about," I began drawing a thread, "predicts how much deliberate practice someone's going to do. They did this cool study where they found the higher grit people had, the more likely they were to undertake deliberate practice."

Bails had liked the grit concept, and saw immediate links to our new draftees trying to make it through their first years in the system, and probably to his own story of graft as a footballer himself.

"But how do we make them gritty then?"

129

"They're still not sure," I was honest, "but there's two possible ways. One is to help them persevere more, which gives them a chance to make the right neural pathways become more ingrained."

"Tick," Bails playfully offered his agreement, giving me a chance to swig my espresso shot.

"Yep. The other is to help them be more passionate, or want it more."

"Well maybe, Paddy," Bails threw an idea out there, "just maybe, if we can show them that its possible – if guys like him become superstars – then they'll be more passionate about the process. *Then* we're on our way."

I offer up a glimmer of hope back in the dull confines of Bails new room. "Most of the stuff in the media about his record now is talking about the way he practices as the key."

There's no magic pill for getting better, I recall Bails saying only days earlier. The analogy was starkly reinforced now with the medication that remained on the table in front of him, the next hurdle in his race against time.

"I've got plenty of thinking time in here," he looked at the prison walls, almost in anger, as he sat down to catch his wind. "The more I think about it," he began once he had enough oxygen, "the more I'm certain. There's a definite advantage in coaching the mental game."

I nodded, without wanting to lead him too much.

"If we can help our guys stay clear." He adjusted the oxygen tubes in his nostrils, which had shifted in the short walk. "Clear and calm under pressure. We'll be miles ahead of the others."

I nodded in agreement, though I didn't need to. He was the pope and I was the priest, already converted.

"Clutch," he said, as clearly and loudly as anything he had uttered so far on this visit. "A tag they all want. You help them go there? They'll do anything for 'ya." At that moment, his voice raspy and his phrases shortened, a picture of Yoda from *Star Wars* filled my head.

"What made the Cats so good?" Bails threw up an example in his now staccato sentences. "All make great decisions, all think the same, 'specially when it gets tight."

"But did they all arrive with that?" I probed, inviting him to go further.

"Nah it takes time, and sometimes it ain't pretty while it's happening. I think some smart dude once said expertise is like a sausage: it never looks good while it's being made."

I laughed. A witty reply about "pricks" or "bread" begged to be made

With Geelong the topic of conversation, I sensed a chance to steer toward another topic I know he knew well: culture. I pounced on the mention of the Geelong team who had become a dynasty in the past few years. "Just on the Cats – when they won their first flag, a lot of credit was given to their cultural change and the leadership there." Bails held up a hand to stop me.

"Just on the Cats," he said with a furrowed brow, "were they hanging shit on someone recently? Maybe us?"

"Not that I heard." I replied, surprised. Some media-friendly trash talk was always a good topic with Bails, so I went with it. "What was it?"

"Nah, must've been someone else." For just a moment, he had resembled a guard dog, vigilant, looking to protect his house. He settled back to hospital mode again. "That's okay. Go on."

"Um," As I marshalled my thoughts to return to the topic, Bails' phone danced as text came in. "That the lovely Caron?" I asked, resigned to the fact the visit might be over soon, just as we were getting to the juicy wisdom again. The culture conversation could wait.

"Yep." He tapped away as he unlocked his phone.

"You got a ripper wife, Bails." I wasn't exaggerating. Caron was one of the favourite partners of everyone on the team. In a growing world of flash celebrity and superficial looks, she was a welcome breath of fresh, natural air. A grounded woman, she was a welcoming female influence for anyone who visited their house for dinner on occasion. Small in stature, what she lacked in height she made up for in smiles and energy. And perhaps thanks to what they had been through together, she usually wore a smile, regardless of the result.

"Where do I get me one of those?" I inquired.

"Off the farm." A sly grin appeared at the corner of his mouth as he scrolled through the text.

I laughed. "She's a country girl, is she?"

He nodded. "Off a pineapple farm in Queensland."

"Right." He texted back a reply – tap, tap, tap on his iPhone. It took him a couple of minutes before he set the phone down.

"So," I began once it would no longer be an interruption, "if she's from a pineapple farm in Queensland, how'd you meet her?"

"Ah," he smiled, looking out the window as if it were a screen that would replay the scene for us. His face had a softer expression now than before.

"Mate of mine," he began, "his mum had bad asthma living in Melbourne during the winter. Every time she went to Queensland for a holiday, she didn't have it. Or she did, a bit wheezy, but eighty percent better. So she went up there, and 'cos they were landscapers, they were looking around to see if there were any reasonable contracts."

He shifted himself up onto the bed now, keen to relive the story.

"Ross's old man was pretty good at what he was doing," he resumed once he had found a comfortable spot, and counted on his fingers, "landscaping, sitting in a chair eating, and watching football. They were his three favourite hobbies."

We both chuckled at that mental picture.

"So they went up there. I went up for a holiday, and Ross says to me, 'I've got this girl you might like' and I say 'Oh right'." His grin widens now. "So I picked her up – he'd told her 'I got this guy you might like' - and we just hit it off from the start. So that was that."

The story was so Dean and Caron - simple, no fuss.

"And when the opportunity came, I'd fly up to Brisbane. A couple of times, I'd fly her down to Melbourne to meet the parents. It just sort of evolved. You know, it was a long-distance relationship, which was good fun – we still had fun and went out and met other people..."

His voice trailed off as another text came in. He read it once, then read it again, contemplating it, and then he read the thing out loud. "'What was I like the other day?'" Frowning slightly, he glanced over at me before returning his attention to the phone. "Not too bad... I suppose." He started tapping away again; when he was done, he held onto the phone. "What were you saying?" he asked me.

"Can't remember," I told him, glancing down at my notes. "Actually..." My eye caught on a doodle. "Oh, you were just talking about how you met Caron."

"Oh yeah. Then it got to a stage in about eighty-nine where I played Geelong in a final in '89. I got reported for hitting Buddha," he laughed at this - he and Gary 'Buddha' Hocking had coached together since and got on extremely well. "Stupid report. I wanted to hit him; I just missed!" That brought on another laugh.

"My season was done, so then I drove my car up to Cairn's, 'cos she was teaching up there on a placement. Spent maybe a month up there? Stayed up there and decided it'd be a good idea if she came back with me to Melbourne to see if we could make something work. So that was it."

He paused, sensing a delicious irony given our earlier discussion about decision-making.

"Some decisions make themselves, Paddy." No grin rested on his lips now, as he tried to remain dry. But the glint in his eye showed how chuffed he was with that call, so many years ago.

I smiled and clapped. "How long had you known her at that point?"

"Oh, 1984 we'd met first time, so we'd known each other a long time. But it was good fun." He stopped talking then, a faint smile creeping back to his face, happy in his memories.

"And the team," I offered a new topic after a short while, "it gives an almost instant social club when you move to a new one, doesn't it?" I thought I would explore the impact a solid community has on people's lives. Instead, like the puppeteers were finally beginning to smile on me, there was a timely knock at the door.

"Hello?" Caron called to greet us as she walked through the open door.

"Hello," I started with enthusiasm, but then broke off as I saw who followed her in. "Hey, Mitch!"

"Hey, mate," Mitch said with a cheery wave.

"Oh, it's just havoc out in the car park," Caron remarked, setting her purse on the floor under the chair closest to the bedside.

"Yeah, it's packed, isn't it!" It had been pretty close to being full when I arrived a little while ago.

"Happy Valentine's Day!" she told her husband, and leaned in for a kiss. I had almost ignored the date, busy being busy, and single. She laid her gift of love on the table: *The Age* and *Inside Football* newspapers – brain food for Bails. His eyes lit up as he reached for them.

"*The Age!*" I exclaimed. "Well played! Proper news."

"Exactly," Caron said with a grin, "not the *Agonizer...* "

"Would you believe there's some good stuff in today's Addy?" I posed the rhetorical question about the local rag, the Adelaide Advertiser. "I read more than one page."

"Oh," Caron played along, clearly not a fan. "Confidential?"

"Ha ha. Nah," I laughed at her reference to the social pages, the kind we both despised. "Started at the back page."

I always turn to the sports pages first – something Bails and I discovered we had in common when we first lived together. The back pages record people's accomplishments & victories more often than not. The front pages are usually dedicated to failures and fears.

We shared a grin as she reached into the plastic bag she held. "Got some grapes for you, too," she told Bails. "And menthol."

"That's a good combination," he said with dry enthusiasm. He pointed to the torn paper bag I had placed on his table soon after entry. "Paddy's bought me some fairy bread."

"Oh, party time?" she laughed as she pulled her chair a bit closer to the bed and sat.

"Last time I came just with the pizza rolls," I said, "and I mentioned to Bails that they had some samples – well, they had fairy breads. So of course, I had some 'cos I thought 'that's brilliant, I'll feel like a kid again here!'."

"And I was quite disappointed that you didn't smuggle any out." The children's party treat - white bread laced with butter and sprinkles - was right up both our alleys. It was neck and neck between the two of us in the competition for who had the sweetest tooth.

I noddeds in concession. "So today, I said 'Can you give me a few of those', and my server, young Natalie..."

"She came to the party!" Caron joined in the excitement. She turned back to Bails. "Got you a shaver, in case you wanted to have a shave. You might look ten years younger!"

Smiling but not adding much, Mitch had hung near the door. Before I could tune in to his discomfort, he had headed back out to the car with Caron's keys to fetch something.

"So what were we saying Paddy?" Bails asked, looking to join Caron into the chat.

"Ah, not much," I replied with a grin, leaving the romantic reminiscing up to him. "Just winding through a few different stories. Actually, now that you're here this one might be a good topic for both of you." I shifted, so Caron could sit next to Bails, now reclined on the bed, and I sat next to her, closer to the window.

"What strikes you most about this situation?" I directed my question to both of them. "With what you're going through right now - being part of a football club versus what might not be there otherwise?"

"Just how quick other people rally around," Bails is quick to respond on this one. "When someone I don't know contacts someone I kinda know, and two days later my wife doesn't need to worry about feeding the boys any more."

Caron nods with a pained smile and the room falls silent. It was a great example of the positive people power we had spoken about a few sessions back and highlighted how attuned he was to that side of things.

"Yeah," she adds, "but that happens in other communities too, you know. At a school, for example. It's just what good communities do, you know?"

I nodded, offering a simple "mmm" to show my agreement.

After a moment, Bails sat up and swung over the side of the bed, careful and deliberate. Excusing himself to have another shot at getting his body going, he shuffled to the toilet.

As the toilet door clicked shut, I turned to talk more superficial talk with Caron, and I could see her face already beginning to contort with emotion as she tried to hold it in.

"It's just not fair," she exhaled. I watched the first tear roll down her cheek, her chin quivering, "after all the shit we've been through."

Proper tears now, flooding out of her eyes, which she was attempting to keep open. The tears continued to come even if she held her breath, so instead she started sobbing. "I don't want to plan all this by myself."

The sorrow was immense. I had felt my emotions tested by what was going on, but nowhere near the depth that Caron or Bev, or Ted, or Todd, or the boys would feel. Watching her curled up on the hospital visitors' chair, I couldn't help but feel a part of her sorrow. As my heart expanded in sympathy, the tears started rolling down my face. One dropped onto my t-shirt.

From the hints I had picked up in conversations to this point with Bails, it was obvious this wasn't going to be a successful fight for Bails. Caron's words suggested it was not going to be a long one either. While the messaging back at the coalface was positive, the clichés about being up for the battle were just a cover-up for what was happening here in this room.

Bails was dying. Fast.

This moment was perhaps the rawest I had faced so far. And even though I was much more comfortable talking in this space now, I hesitated to open it right up with Caron. Bails had agreed to hand me some power in our conversations, and to open up his emotions. Caron hadn't, and I didn't want to make her go anywhere she didn't want to herself.

"And to a good person." She continued to cry, emotions that she kept locked away most of the time pouring out in her sobs and her tears. Her positivity was important to Bails, and she didn't want to burden him more with her inner turmoil.

As I watched her suffer in silence, I felt torn between the urge to hug her and wanting to not prompt further tears. In the end, all I muttered was a true statement, that recognized my understanding of how lonely she felt.

"I can't begin to imagine, Caron."

She began catching her breath and wiping the tear tracks from her cheeks.

"I'm fine." The tough country girl was still here.

The silence following her dismissal of the grief settled things a little. I allowed it to sit until Caron was ready to take the conversation wherever she might want it to go. The paper was the first thing her eyes alighted on, and she took it to safer ground with another joke about the social pages. I was more than happy to follow her lead.

Soon after, Bails reappeared, and I sensed the time was right to let the couple be a couple. Not the most romantic environment, but anything positive was worth amplifying right now.

"I'll let you guys be," I said as I stood, "Valentine's day and all."

"What have you got planned?" Caron asked like a curious mum.

"Nothing planned," I replied. "No point planning if you got no one to plan with! I'll go home and work till bedtime. So feel free to have a chocolate in my honour!"

We all laughed, and I left the lovebirds to be together.

Breakfast With Bails

| | | |

About a month after being spotted in a country pub with his pants around his ankles, serial bad-boy Bernie Vince sat with Bails in his office. To mark the formality of the occasion, Bernie had kept his shorts on this time.

The media interest that accompanied the story was akin to the kidnapping of a child, given the level of coverage devoted to it. The hysteria had since died down, and the official sanctions since passed. The remaining conditions of showing remorse and undergoing some rehabilitation were to meet with Bails or myself every other week.

"I swear mate!" Bernie pleaded with a grin. Bails sat opposite him with his eyebrows raised in suspicion, a small knowing grin at the corners of his open mouth.

"So you're telling me you're doing it?" Bails probed. "Every day?" He had the knowing look of a prison warden who used to be a criminal himself.

"I've done it every day this week!"

"Fourteen times? Every morning?"

"Every morning." Bernie was adamant. "I'll take a photo of the marks on my bedroom wall if you want proof."

"Nah, no need for that Bern, I trust you. I just find it hard to believe that it's working. Hard to scrub off a leopard's spots, you know."

As a small lab experiment, Bails had decided to test out some of the latest theory in practice. With a test case of one, we were trialling some of the research around habit change that we had discussed over so many breakfasts and coffees. He would give Bernie a simple task to see if his

139

level of self-awareness and ability to stick to a task would change. The task? Do something – whatever Bernie wanted – fourteen times, every morning. Fourteen pushups. Fourteen squats. Fourteen stretches.

"You remember why I picked fourteen, Bern?" Bails probed, testing how well he understood what he was doing.

"To remind me of where we were last year." The Crows had finished fourteenth in the season before we arrived – the worst in their history.

"That's right. I want you to remember how embarrassing that was every single day, so you don't waste a moment of the time you get to make up for it this year. Keep you thinking about something that will motivate you from inside, you know, 'cos it's hard to stay focused that much. Are you sure you..."

"If I wanted to lie to 'ya I woulda said I was doing it from the start," Bernie cut him off with a smile. "And I've told you when I forgot. I let you down almost every day that first week!"

Bernie had struggled to find something that worked at first. But now he was throwing a tennis ball against a wall and catching it – sharpening his reflexes – fourteen times, daily.

"Okay. I'm not doing this just for shits and giggles Bern. I just want you to be better than I was."

Bernie nodded. "I know."

Even after he had moved interstate to a new team - even after the coach who rode him had fallen ill and passed away - Bails' little tricks stuck, and they made Bernie better.

TACKLING
WE TALK ABOUT ADVERSITY & RESILIENCE

"Hello?" I pushed into the room, but Caron was the only person there, sitting in a visitor's chair. Bails was nowhere to be seen. "Has he done a runner?" I joked.

"Nah." She nodded toward the closed door on the other side of the room. "He's just trying his luck in the toilet."

I glanced at the table, pushed away from the side of the bed at a bit of an angle. There was a steaming cup of some hot beverage there already. "You beat me to it, looks like," I observed, referring not only to the cup on the table but the two in my hands.

"That's a hot chocolate," she told me, pointing toward the table.

"Well, I got a skinny mocha for him as well as mine, so you can have it if you want." I'd intended it for Bails, but if Caron had bought him a hot chocolate, odds are that's what he'd prefer. She knew him better than anyone.

Bails walked out from the toilet, drying his hands on a paper towel before tossing it into the trashcan.

"You go there," Caron told me, waving away the mocha. "I'm just sitting here."

"Okay." I sat in another visitor's chair, a little closer to the bed. "I'm right with my short black, so honestly, you can have the mocha," I offered, extending the frothy, steaming coffee towards her.

"Okay," she relented, rolling her eyes in mock exasperation, "I'll have it."

"I'll mop up whatever you leave," I assured her, "and I also smuggled the banana bread in, which I'm more than happy to help out on as well."

"I noticed that, yes," Bails said with some enthusiasm as we settled in. "So we're all ready to go today, are we?" he asked, turning towards me.

He seemed in much better condition today than on my previous visit, with more energy as well as better mobility. I might have taken his question as a signal of enthusiasm for my visit, but for the fact I knew full well what he was referring to. Game day.

"Yeah," I began, "bit of tension."

With the first match for the year on later in the day, albeit just a practice game, a little tension wasn't such a bad thing. Given it was against the cross-town rivals, Bails' old team in Port Adelaide, there would be plenty who would play for keeps.

"Sando's changed already in the last..." I stopped to do some mental arithmetic. "When did I see you last? A week ago?"

Bails looked up at the roof, almost mimicking my own puzzled facial expression. Caron gave a definitive nod, and that was good enough for me to move on.

"It's a different—" I paused, not wanting to overstate things, "a different life. As you would know better than most, Bails. Once games come around..."

"True." He was nodding as he fiddled with something under his bedside table. "Can you put this down, Paddy? I think if you loosen that there," he pointed toward a metal clasp of some sort, "you can just push the table top down from the top."

"Sure thing." I bent forward to see how to work the thing. A quick twist, a bit of pressure in the center of the tabletop, and we were back on topic. "There?"

"A bit lower," Bails instructed. I obliged, and dropped the table another half an inch. "There. Thanks Paddy."

"No prob," I sat back down. "Yeah, so it's a bit of a different buzz."

"It's all right. Playing on the edge, it's not a bad thing. As long as he doesn't overdo it for a practice match." Bails took a sip of his hot chocolate and set the cup on the table. "He won't do it – he's a good coach. He's got a good feel."

The two coaching minds in the room talked tactics for a little: who would play in the 6? Where do we rest Danger? How do we use the newest toys we acquired in free agency? Caron's eyes looked down at a magazine to avoid becoming glazed over.

"How many are they expecting to roll up at the game this weekend?" Caron joined back in the conversation when there was a long enough lull to redirect the chat.

"Yeah, I dunno." I took a sip of my coffee; it had cooled to just the right temperature. Being a short black, it was gone in one gulp.

Bails nodded again. "They'll pull a few."

"I haven't heard any official numbers, but I'm expecting eight to ten thousand."

Silence for a bit then, as we drank our respective beverages and cut into the snack I had supplied.

"Doesn't look like a bad day outside," Bails offered through a mouthful of banana bread.

"Nah, it's a good day for it," I replied, glancing toward the window. "Windy, not sunny."

"Yeah," Bails paused, and then took the opportunity to grab the wheel. "I got a big day today." With that, he segued into something he was as excited about as the game: new visitors. "Got Blair Hartley coming to see me."

"Oh, really?" I asked, intrigued.

"Yeah. Parks. I think he's dropping in. Barry Prendergast, who I worked with at Melbourne. All round for our game, and they all text, not together, each saying, 'Can I drop in?' I'm thinking, 'What's goin' on?' and then I realise they're all coming over to watch us play." He's buzzed at the visitors from his past teams: Blair from the Bombers, Parks from the Power, Barry from Melbourne. "And Crippa – Jason Cripps – from Port."

"Ah, you would've worked with Crippa at Port, of course." I had grown up in the same region of Melbourne as Crippa, and watched him play with my older brother in rep squads as juniors. We had even worked together for a short while. Small world, this business.

"Yeah, a few years."

"Where's Crippa these days? Port?" I couldn't recall if he'd moved on from there or not.

"Yeah, he's list manager," Bails answered.

"Yeah, 'cos I remember I ran into him at the coaches' conference last year; for some reason I thought he was back in Melbourne."

"Yeah," Caron said, "he's based in Melbourne. That was part of it – his wife wanted to get back there I think. So they negotiated and he sort of created the position in Melbourne."

"They needed it like that though," Bails added.

"They didn't have one?" I was more than a little surprised at that.

"Oh, this is a couple of years ago. They sorta'... it wasn't a separate job, it came under a few other things."

"Like football manager?"

"Yeah, it might've been a little bit of Peter Rohde, it was a little bit of Parks, and a little bit of Crippa, but nobody owned it. So, they just saw that that was a big hole in their structure. They just thought they had to find the right person, whereas...," he shrugged, "they found him. He was sitting right under their nose. He's been pretty good from what I hear, good pedigree: done the leadership stuff, he's coached, been a runner, and he's a good person."

I nodded, recalling the high level facilitation skills I'd seen first hand. "Be a good GM eventually, wouldn't he? Or is that a step sideways from a list manager?"

"Yeah, I dunno," Bails pondered the path. "I'm not sure where you go from personnel, unless you move to another team. I don't know what the next move is from there. Might be GM. Can't see it going anywhere else."

"At least it's in something he loves though, so that's a good thing," I noted, as much to finish the conversation as anything. Bails instead offered a tempting lead to go deeper.

"The game can take over your life if you love it too much. It can do funny things to people."

"In a good or a bad way?" I quizzed him for more info on such an unexpected statement, made even more profound coming from someone who had given their life to the game.

"Oh," he leant back, perhaps only now becoming aware of what his statement might suggest given his own story, "I don't think you have any bad experiences. You have a few that disappoint you, that you'd like to change, but..."

He hesitated, searching for another way to explain it. I have to jump in here.

"So wait," I hold up a hand, almost unsure if I heard him right. "You wouldn't look at the last few years you've been through and say any of them are bad experiences? No hard feelings?" My eyebrows were about as high as they could go.

"I only hold grudges against a few people." Bails made sure he balanced his earlier statement about letting things go. He was never one to lie. "Might only be a couple."

Bails cleared his throat, almost in press conference mode now. Careful crafting of words now. "What I mean is, you only get experience by doing the job. By getting your hands dirty. Sometimes those experiences are bad, sometimes they're good. But I don't think you can sit there and say, 'That was a horrendous experience, I didn't learn anything from it.' I wouldn't look at it that way. Not even with the experiences I've had—and I've had some horrendous ones."

Caron nodded, solemn but firm. In another place and time, she might've offered witness with an "Amen!"

"Would I prefer to have not had them?" Bails was clearing the air now. "Absolutely. You'd prefer not to have them. But you did, you experienced them, you went through them, so does it make you a bit stronger? Or does it make your understanding much better? Or do you get a better insight into people? Yep. Yep. And yep."

The buzz of the hospital life outside seemed muted now, dwarfed by the significance of this moment for Bails. For the first time, I heard him talk without any hint of malice about the slings and arrows he had suffered at the hands of the game. He had given this idea lip service when I had visited him during his suspension, or once he was back, wanting to move on. But only now did he sound like he meant it.

"Now you've got a much better insight into people and how they think," he concluded, matter-of-factly. "Well done. That's your prize for getting through."

Maybe his current struggle gave it perspective. Maybe he just had so much time to think. Whatever it was, I could almost hear it in his voice. Had he really let go of the past?

Back in the café at the club, we were well into our second or third coffee of the day. It was quiet, as the players had not returned to begin pre-season yet, so coaches could enjoy a little more time to catch up.

"Enough about my trip, Paddy. What sort of mischief did you get up to on yours?" Bails asked once he had swigged the remainder of his mocha.

"You know me Bails," I smiled, "all business." He had loved the stories I had shared with him when we first lived together of modern day strategies – albeit unsuccessful ones to date – for finding love. I had nothing new for him today.

"I accidentally met some pretty cool people, though," I went straight to the highlights. "I thought I might get to meet Duckworth – the Grit lady – but she was busy. Instead, I got some one on one time with this guy named Seligman."

"Oh yeah?" Bails played along, oblivious to the names. "What's he do?"

"Well I didn't know it, but he was maybe even better to meet with than the Grit guru."

"Why's that?" Bails began to lean back in his chair, a sign he might be moving on in a second.

"Well he found the keys to helping people handle adversity better," I summed up as quick as I could. "And they've trained the army how to do it too."

Bails leaned back forward again, checking if he had heard right. "What?"

"Yep," I confirmed he had. "He's basically the godfather of this whole different field – positive psychology. They initially did it for mental health, but found performance benefits too."

"Like what?"

"Well," I reached for the most relevant anecdote I could think of. "He did this cool study with elite swimmers in the 80s – 50 of them, from the US. Back when Matt Biondi was the man."

"Biondi!" Bails exclaimed. "I remember him. Big dude."

"I don't," I replied with a wry grin, "but I'll take your word for it! Anyway they tricked them into thinking they swam a slow time on their pet event. They told em it was a shit time, swim it again."

"So what?"

"Well they had already checked the swimmers to see who was optimistic and who wasn't. The swimmers baseline levels of optimism predicted how they would handle the 'setback' of a poor performance, even better than their ability or their own coach's gut feel - which they also measured."

"So the optimistic ones bounced back & swam faster," Bails tried to sum it up, "and the others didn't?"

"Pretty much," I nodded, happy with the quick synopsis from Bails. "Best part is the results hold up in team environments, including NBA and MLB teams."

"Really!" Bails' excitement was genuine, and his nodding showed the research jived with his experience. "Yeah it makes sense, even to an old fart like me. You look at guys who aren't that way – they just give up easier. They're automatically at a disadvantage when the shit hits the fan, cos they don't respond the right way. And you said they trained it?" Bails checked, bringing it back to our job.

"Yep – more than 20,000 officers in the US army, a last count."

"Well then Paddy," Bails smiled and leaned in as if sharing a secret plan, "maybe that's how we justify the next set of trips to the bosses: even if we got nothing this time, we just need to be optimistic and go again!"

I laughed, and Bails turned to a couple of die-hard fans who had found their way into the café on a random off-season day. He slipped straight from business mode to chatting socially, like a well-trained politician, ignoring the fact people have treated you poorly in the past. Maybe these supporters will be different.

"Some experiences I've had I wouldn't wanna go through again," back in room 440, Bails rolled on. "But unfortunately I have. And you try to learn and pick up a few things, and then push the rest of it out of your brain so it just doesn't keep circulating in your head."

"So are you saying nothing's bad," I tried to sum up the underlying lesson here, which might be helpful to the guys back at the club, "at least, as long as you can take things from it?"

"I think there are things that are bad and you can still take something from it," Bails clarified, "but I don't think you should let it define you. I don't think it should influence everything you do. Think about it: what if someone from Melbourne rang someone from Adelaide and said, 'Dean Bailey's a dickhead. He's no good, he can't do this, he can't do that, he can't coach, he can't talk.' Just bagged the shit out of me. What if the person from Adelaide listened to the person from Melbourne, and took it as truth?"

It was a rhetorical question, but he paused here to allow my brain to follow the path he was laying out.

"Nothing I can do about that!" He huffed a mucous-filled laugh. "As soon as I walk in the door, he'll look at me a certain way, without giving me an opportunity to just be who I am, not treat me as I treat you, you know? Some people have preconceived ideas of others before they walk in. I think one thing experience teaches you is that you shouldn't walk in with any preconceived ideas about anyone, 'cos they're always gonna surprise you. And more often than not, they surprise you in a good way."

I was genuinely surprised by how positive he was about what to expect from people, especially given the past few years. He had endured a litany of slings and arrows, from enough antagonists to fill a roster of an entire football team. *How can you still expect the best of people after that?* I wondered to myself, trying to think of an example from my own life. Bails beat me to it.

"You know," he looked straight at me, "I didn't know anything about you until we lived together, even though it was only a short time. But the mental side of the game has always been of interest to me, I've just never had a decent chunk of time to get into it and understand it. I like the development part of it,

149

too. So having you come in was very interesting and unexpected. I liked that."

I smiled, proud and humbled at the same time.

"It's interesting," I responded to his compliment. "I remember the first time I came to visit you in the hospital. I was thinking back to when we met: I knew a bit of your background, and I'd seen you in pressers when you're under the pump more than anything. And then the bloke that met me at the airport and that I lived with for a bit, was just... completely different. It was a surprise, and a good surprise, to meet the real you. Not the bloke who was under pressure, but just a normal guy who happens to know a lot of shit about football and people. And who can eat."

"I miss that appetite," he lamented.

I chuckled. "Are you eating better now that you're back here?"

"Oh, yeah I guess so. I was saying to Caron, mighta been yesterday that I hit the cheesy mite scroll pretty hard. And a pizza roll, which is quite good, 'cos it put a bit of weight on me."

There was a lull in conversation. The newspaper on the floor beside the bed caught my eye, reminding me of something I'd read that morning. "Is that today's or yesterday's?" I asked Bails, pointing to it.

"Today's, I think."

"You should read the double page spread in the middle on Rhonda Cornum. Did I mention the U.S. army general that I've got coming in to speak to the leaders and coaches?" Bails nodded his head while Caron shook hers. "So I went and checked her out."

They both had a good chuckle at that and I just stared at them for a moment until it dawned on me what I'd said.

"Well, not checked her out," I clarified, "I went and watched her speak! She's not my type." I laughed then, too. "They had a double page spread on her in the paper yesterday. It's quite interesting. It's quite an impressive bio – she's a surgeon, or a neurologist, so she was in the army as a medical officer. Shot down in a Blackhawk when they were going to rescue someone, held as a prisoner of war. Raped, tortured, shot at a couple of times, and then she got out. It's pretty unusual for a woman to find herself in that spot and survive."

"She must have balls," Caron remarked.

"Yeah, well the way she described it, to be honest, she said there wasn't much choice. She looked at it and thought, 'Well, I could be dead.' That was her thought in that moment."

"So that was the other option," Caron commented, looking impressed, "so she's like 'I'll just deal with it.'"

"Yep. She got cancer, as well – once she became a general. She's an outlier, though. Her attitude to everything is almost...," I searched for the right adjective and settled on the closest I could find, "inhuman. She's got a positive attitude to everything, like she's about to die and she thinks 'Well, at least I'm gonna die doing something I'm proud of.' Then she's getting raped, and she thinks 'Well, at least I'm not dying.' She's just able to get a positive out of everything. But it was good for the board too, 'cos I think they'll be happy to support some serious programs for that stuff now."

"Mmmm. Good. Yeah, they'll like that. Toughness."

"Yeah." I could see the story was as engaging for them as it was for me. "It's quite amazing. Her experience since in setting up the resilience training stuff in the army is just as amazing. She's one of those people you could just sit with and let her tell stories for hours."

"Stories about resilience and toughness?" Bails checked to see if he was on the same page.

"Yup." I confirmed that he was. "The best part is that it's trainable, and it's simple. It's all based on that optimism stuff I told you about at Swedish Tarts when we came back."

"How'd you find her?" Bails asked.

151

"When I went to Philadelphia in October to visit the Eagles, I also got to meet with Karen Reivich at the same time. She built the resilience training that they deliver to the army, and she mentioned this general while she told me about it. I didn't think much of it at the time, 'cos you know, who's gonna get access to a retired military general. Next thing I know they've come out here for a well-being symposium. So right now, Martin Seligman's here, as well as a couple of the other bigwigs in that field, and she's come out as a guest speaker. So I said, 'Let's try and rope her in while she's here.' It's much sexier to sell to the coaches and the executive, rather than getting a psychologist in."

"No doubt." You could tell he liked the sound of it. "I've always thought that you gotta remain upbeat – doesn't mean you'll win next time, but if you give up you'll definitely lose. No, that's good. Some powerful messages in there."

He paused for a moment, sipping from his not-so-hot chocolate before starting up again. "And the boys are going all right?"

"Yeah," I replied, with perhaps a little less enthusiasm than previous responses. "There's a little bit of guys complaining about too many meetings and all that sort of stuff."

"The blokes who are in the squad and don't have to worry about their position?"

I thought about it for half a second. "Nope. Guys who aren't playing, but won't have to worry about their spot once they're back. That'll sort itself out. I've got a couple of extra groups running that finish in a couple of weeks, so it will be much easier after that."

He nodded, nothing to add here.

"I spoke to the club about Mitch, as well."

"Oh, yeah? And?" Not overt in his interest, but I could tell he wanted this locked in sooner rather than later.

"Well, there's still that role I spoke to you about – that hybrid thing – but turns out one of the other cadet slots has opened up. They sacked one."

"Oh did they? Who was that?"

"Dunno," I shook my head. "I just spoke to Nick about it as I left here the other day. So he's got a full role now."

"I think Mitch is meeting with him Monday," Caron mentioned, looking from Bails to me and back again.

"Oh, that's good." An understated smile made Bails a picture of pride and relief. "That's better than I thought, to be honest."

"Me, too!" I joined his smile.

"Yeah," Caron added, her smile making it a full house. "Be good for his confidence, too. But he'll have to get better at the speaking."

"Talking, communicating," Bails agreed.

"Yeah, 'cos he's not like Darcy, like that." She sipped at her coffee.

"They're chalk and cheese in some ways like that, aren't they?" I observed.

"Oh, they are. So different." Another sip of mocha as she thought about her sons. "Mitchell's a lot more sensitive and more there for me. Darcy just keeps himself busy. With Darcy, it's a lot of bravado, though. I think, deep down, he's a bit like Tex in that way, he's soft and kind hearted, you know?"

"Yeah." I didn't know about Darcy, but I knew about Tex.

"That's just how you get through, though. I say to Mitchell: confidence means a lot. A lot of people, that's how they survive, by just having that..."

"That confidence." Bails finished Caron's sentence for her.

"It's interesting," I pick up the thread, "because the General was talking about confidence in the resilience training. True confidence, if you strip it all back, is just about coping strategies: thinking that you will be able to deal with what comes up, that it will work out all right. But in the army, a typical coping strategy is just beat your chest and pretend you're okay."

"Yeah, I'm a he-man, yeah." Caron recognised the response, army background or not.

"Or just don't think or talk about it." I went on. "But at some stage you have to find a way to get it out of your head or to feel good about it, so that's how people end up drinking, or doing drugs."

"Yeah, otherwise they get sick, or end up with mental illness, if they don't get it out or make themselves feel better." Caron was quite well attuned to this topic.

"They end up doing something stupid. I'm surprised how much of an issue it seemed to be for them in the army, given they're all supposed to be so disciplined."

"What sort of things?" Bails asked.

"Well, they have what they call 'Indiscipline Issues.' As in alcohol abuse, substance abuse, sexual abuse, people going AWOL. If they're in Korea, for example, they're based in another Asian country on deployment, where prostitution is a pretty well run, prevalent industry. The guys will go AWOL for a night, just so they can go root some Thai hooker. But for the army, that's a big problem: if you're on deployment, we can't have you disappearing for a night. We don't know where the hell you are!"

Everyone laughs at the simple example, or my mischievous grin. Either way, the laughter in this room is welcome. I roll on with the example.

"But this turns out to be an issue that they have to deal with in the army, along with others. Guys will go missing, or abuse alcohol or have suicidal thoughts. The extremes that we have that end up all over the paper - which are pretty rare - are more common in the army just by sheer weight of numbers, if nothing else."

"Yeah, right," Bails said, finishing his hot chocolate. "And it's all about them not dealing with the stress properly. Imagine: 'You felt like you were gonna die today?' That's pretty stressful."

"Pretty heavy," Caron said with a shudder.

"Exactly," I nodded, "especially for a twenty-year-old kid to handle. But you can't go out and drink to turn down your nerves, or you can't go root your life away to make yourself feel better, 'cos you'll get herpes and we'll have to send you back home."

"Or have three Vietnamese kids running around," Caron quipped and we all laughed in unison again.

"That is full on, isn't it?" Bails said. "Saying to Caron that last night I woke up twice during the night, this thing – this little gas thing," he gestured toward the clear plastic tubes in his nose. "I don't know how, but I flicked it out of my nose, and I didn't know. I'm still sleeping, sleeping, and all of a sudden I wake up a bit sweaty and a bit coughy. 'Where's me gas thing?' Couldn't find it. I'm crawling around, feeling around. Anyways, I find it, and I stick it back in, and I go back to sleep, but only after I calm down from the stress. Shitting myself that I might not be able to breathe."

"You are very twitchy at the moment," Caron said to him, trying to avoid the picture of him taking his final breath. She turns to me to explain. "It's because of the drugs."

"Big twitches," he agreed. "Yeah, the drugs they've got me on the last week or two are giving me some real big twitches. Sometimes I almost jump up out of my seat. My arms have gone up or a big karate chop to the tube or something."

"Are you having vivid dreams?"

"Nah, not really."

"Mm, bummer," Caron said suggestively, then broke into an infectious laugh that we all caught.

"Yeah," Bails returned to the topic at hand when we settled, "it's weird. Even during the day I'll find myself twitching a bit – watch my fingers go crazy. It's a strange existence."

Strange indeed. A silence fell again as we each contemplated that. Bails turned to look out the window while I had another piece of banana bread and Caron finished her mocha; as it turned out, it wasn't too much for her, after all.

She turned to me after she put the cup down and asked, "How's your house hunting going, Paddy?"

"It's messy, Caron." I grimaced. The question forced me to think about my own domestic situation, which was also a strange existence right now thanks to a messy breakup.

"I'm looking, too," she shared.

That startled me out of my own self analysis. "Yeah?" I asked her, glancing over at Bails. This was a clear admission that things were going to change significantly for her and the boys, sooner rather than later.

"Yeah, but I don't know," she confirms, "I just can't find that right one. Takes so much time, too."

"Yeah, I haven't got a heap of time, either," I share her pain, "but mine's complicated by girl issues."

"Mm? Well, I don't have that." She laughed again. "Just do your own thing. Buy your own and pay for it all yourself." Good motherly advice.

"Oh, nah, that's not the issue. Be good if that was the issue."

"Paddy's the issue, Caron. No one can live with him!" Bails, cracks the tension with a straight face, deadpan as always.

"That could be it!" I laughed. For a moment I turned inward, considering what he had joked about, and the element of truth in it. Sitting with Bails all this time, a man known for his selflessness and giving, had made me all too aware of how self-absorbed I had become since my playing days. It would've made me damn hard to live with, and I realised that if I didn't change soon, it would be a long, lonely life ahead.

"You gotta stop making those pasta bricks to try and entertain people," he bought me back to the room with a joke at my expense. In the first week of living together, I had attempted

156

to cook my standard pasta dish as a thank you. He never asked me to cook again.

"Those pasta brick squares you produced when we were living together," he held up his hands like he was trying to lift something massive, yet small, and we all laughed pretty hard at that.

"I'm thinking of building my own house using those," I told him, setting us all off once more.

"Mm, you probably could," Bails said, still chuckling. "You could certainly make a dog house out of it." We were all laughing again now.

"It's still in your fridge, isn't it?"

"Gee, I hope so." More laughter from us all, but this time it seemed a bit too much for Bails as the laughter dissolved into coughs.

We go on to talk about all sorts of things, none related to death or hard stuff. We revel in the good stuff for a change, and for a short while our worries - mine about small things, Caron's about big things, and Bails' about the biggest thing of all - don't seem as big.

SCRIMMAGE THREE

DEFENCE

| | | |

As I passed Bails in his normal habitat at work in the preseason of 2013, something seemed odd. He wasn't the study of concentration he often appeared to be when one caught him alone in his office between 7am and 7pm. Rather than hovering over his screen coding, or leaning back in his chair absorbing a video that would inform his input to a coaches' meeting later that day, he just sat and stared at the wall.

"Looks like you need a triple shot in the Mocha I'm about to get you, mate," I joked, leaning on his door frame.

The joke sailed over his head like a straight shot from the most accurate kicker. He didn't laugh; he didn't even look up. He was deep in thought on more pressing matters.

"Nah, that won't help. The AFL are riding me, Paddy," he offered, with no more detail to explain the specific riding technique they were using on him.

"This about the tanking thing?" I probed, not knowing where this might take the conversation.

His response came thick and fast, as he related his version of the AFL investigation process held into his actions as coach of Melbourne.

It seemed to Bails that he was being questioned - no, interrogated - on the nuances of growing wheat crops by a couple of bread makers. Brett Clothier and Abraham Haddad were career administrators within the AFL. Clothier had been the 'Manager of Competition Integrity' since 2008 - the first person in Australia to hold such a position - with responsibilities around gambling, match-fixing, salary cap, and the draft. Haddad was employed by the AFL in early 2012 - in the new role of 'Intelligence Co-ordinator' - to oversee the league's new data system designed to monitor suspect behaviour of any AFL footballer, coach, or official. Both had outstanding legal pedigrees before working at the AFL - one as a legal counsel, the other as a tactical intelligence operative for police - but neither had much experience in teaching, coaching, or developing football talent.

"Hang on – this day, you only had 40 interchange. Surely that suggests you were intentionally tanking and wanting to lose a game."

"No, you hang on," Bails responded, incredulous. "You're totally ignoring the context – we had a player who went down in the first 5 minutes."

"What does that mean?" the interrogators responded in kind.

"Well, it means we have to limit our interchanges so we could still be running later in the day." Exasperated.

Weeks had gone by, and a second round of keystone cops questioning, with still no progress. Finally, on Christmas Eve, the AFL had served three folios of complex legal documents on his doorstep, with only a few short weeks to prepare a response. The deadline was 25th January.

Then in mid-January, with a rush, the AFL became very keen to see Bails prior to the deadline to get it resolved ASAP. A call from the League's 2nd in command, Gillon McLachlan, had Bails' alarm bells ringing. Clothier had been on record previously saying that some investigations were fast tracked due to concerns over damage to the AFL's Integrity.

Bails immediately called his lawyer, Chris Pollard, in a worried state - despite the hot January day, the sweat on his brow was more related to nerves than climate.

"I've got Gillon McLachlan on the phone," Bails says, "and he wants me to meet him in Adelaide."

"What?" came the confused reply at the other end. The strangest thing perhaps was the direct contact, rather than going through the lawyer as would be normal procedure in a case like this.

"He's going to be in Adelaide tomorrow, and he wants me to go meet him at his uncle's offices."

Bails rang McLachlan back after a short chat with Pollard.

"Chris Pollard is acting for me." Silence in response. "I want him to be there."

Pause. "Ok then, I'll go back to Melbourne." With his staccato response and the ensuing deep exhalation, McLachlan made it clear he was not pleased with this disruption to his intended plan. "We'll give you a ticket to come over to Melbourne, and you can bring Chris."

And so it was that on the Friday before the Australia Day long weekend, Bails met Chris at his Melbourne offices, and they then played host to the future CEO of the AFL.

McLachlan, dressed in a full suit, was ready for the seriousness of this discussion. Lawyer by trade, he matched the attire of Bails legal representative. Dean, with no prettiness and all about the business at hand, had dressed in thongs, t-shirt, a cap, and a pair of cargo shorts.

"Dean, we want to protect you," McLachlan laid it on thick once the help had left. "We've got the others – Schwab, Connolly. They've confessed. Got them. The club's in trouble. But mate, we want to protect you, so we want to put an offer to you."

He paused for effect as if building the anticipation at the end of season ceremony.

"And that offer is 16 weeks of suspension."

"We'll think about that," Pollard replied on Dean's behalf, "but we haven't done anything wrong. There's still the option to take this to the Supreme Court because this is all bullshit. The brief you've given us is all bullshit. There're four charges you've laid, and you know you're not going to get up on at least three 'cos the evidence is bullshit. It's a joke."

Bails stared straight at McLachlan, his counsel having called bullshit on his behalf. McLachlan glared back. The final table in the World Series of Poker had nothing on the ice cold faces locking eyes across this table.

"So if you have the others," Pollard continued his offensive, "then why haven't you charged them already?"

"I'm not here to talk about that."

"I'll tell you what I think the reason is," Pollard pressed it home. "Aside from being a disappointing CEO at Melbourne, Schwab is also a director of the holding company of the gambling license at the Bentleigh Club, which Melbourne owns. Let's say, hypothetically, if you charge Melbourne OR Schwab, under the gambling laws the license would be taken away. Meaning financially, Melbourne would fall over. And that's not the biggest domino either - with one team gone, the almighty AFL would be in breach of their broadcasting rights with only 17 teams there to play. Bails is the only one you can go after without shooting yourself in the foot."

The battle lines had been marked, McLachlan brushed off the lawyer and eyeballed Dean as he stood to leave. He wasn't here to discuss league policy or interests. It had also become clear he wasn't here to negotiate, more just to make the league's stance crystal clear.

"Dean, I suggest you take this, because if you don't," putting his hand on Dean's shoulder and fixing him with a steely gaze, "you'll never work in football again in your life."

Satisfied that the look on Bails' face showed he fully understood the weight of his words, McLachlan headed for the door.

"Hey Gil," Bails called over his shoulder as McLachlan reached the door, and then turned to face his nemesis. "I'm not a cheat. I know that for sure, and I won't pretend I am just for you to save face. So Nah, we're not gonna' accept," Bails replied sternly. "Sharpen your pencil and come back to us pal."

"I've made my recommendation to the Commission," McLachlan countered, "and we can't alter that – it's too late because they meet on Monday. You either accept it, or this goes all the way."

And with that, Bails was left with a long weekend to ponder his future in the game he loved. He would feel the pressure of McLachlan's hand on his shoulder, and the words that came with it, every second.

TRAINING

BLOCK THREE

SESSION 7
GOALS
WE TALK ABOUT MEANING & PURPOSE

A couple of days after the first trial game, I headed back to the hospital to debrief with Bails. Before hopping in the lift up to the fourth floor, I check if he still has any cravings left.

> Just downstairs mate, you want a mocha /
> hot choc / anything?

His reply was simple and indicated his appetite wasn't what it used to be.

> Hot choc / medium

"Can you put those blinds down for me, Paddy?" Bails asked me the moment I walked into the room. Sunlight came through the window in fiery streams, making it difficult to see.

"Sure thing," I told him. I set the hot chocolate down on his table and stepped over to lower the blinds. "Bought you some chocolate, although I'm not sure what your appetite's like."

"Not too bad. Not too bad," he said, sounding out of breath, almost as though he'd been running. "What's goin' on?"

"Um, everyone's pretty happy with how things started," I told him as I pulled a chair closer and sat. "It's not a real match and it wasn't real teams that played, but much happier to be in our position than in Port's. You spoke to Walshy at all?"

"Yeah, he was in here yesterday. Phil and Buddha came in, said G'Day. Ah, they didn't have anything more to add than that.

Walshy said we looked sharp, they looked flat. He said we looked big. I said we lost kilos since last year; we're running much better this year. He just said we were pretty good. He said they know a bit more about how we're playing now, but he said you boys get that, too. So, I think on the balance of things, he was impressed with what we did, anyways."

Breathless as he sounded, it didn't seem to slow him down much this morning. But sitting closer now, his appearance was striking – more pale and drawn than I had seen him, with an accumulation of mess around his mouth, presumably from the constant coughing.

"You got a bit on your chin there, mate." I grabbed up a couple of tissues from the box on the windowsill and handed them to him so he could wipe the saliva away. I returned to my chair.

"Oh, thanks." He held on to the tissue, maybe keeping it for later, instead of tossing it right away. "Boys been back training yet or what?"

"They had a flush yesterday, but they haven't touched the ball since the game. Got tactical and skills session tomorrow and then main Friday." I sipped at my chocolate.

"How's last night?"

"Um..." I hesitate for a moment, until I recall what he's referring to. "Oh, I didn't go. Player Sponsor thing?"

"Yeah, some sort of presentation."

"Nah. Didn't go – not my bag, those sort of things. Been such a busy week for the key guys who gotta do everything. Sando's been super busy."

"Oh, has he?" Surprise was evident in his voice. "What's he busy with?"

"Oh, he's just getting pulled here, there, and everywhere with management stuff more than actual coaching."

"By who?"

"Lemme think... they've had a thing last night, Channel Seven filming Thursday arvo, Friday's the golf day."

"Golf day for who?"

"The sponsors. This week's the busiest of the lot, so it sticks out like dogs balls right now. But, in general, he just needs a bit more of a PA – what Mocha used to do. Making sure of his timetable, so if we shift something half an hour, Sando doesn't have to run to each guy and let them know, but everyone gets it communicated to them. We had a good chat about it yesterday, put some things in place so that we free him up to do a bit more coaching. He is getting more time with the coaches though, so that's good."

"You might wanna ask him to give you his schedule for the week or something." Bails leaned forward here, as if divulging a state secret that only those on the inside would know. "Senior coaches, Paddy, are notorious for picking up a little bit here, a little bit there. I'll put that in, and all of a sudden I've got too many of these things I gotta do."

"Oh, you mean like as in an extra appearance?" I hadn't thought about that, but it made some sense.

"Yeah," he followed up with an example, "he might do a favor for his wife. Which, you know, is a choice that he makes. Or the coach could want to promote something. Toyota might get him to go and do this thing that we didn't know about, which he wants to do on a Friday night. So get him to show you his calendar for the month, 'cos that'll give you an idea of what he's got booked. He should only be working on things that deliver wins. Period. See, next month he can't be doing too much..." He paused for a moment to catch his breath. "He can't be doing too much personal stuff. It's the cost of the job."

"Yeah, okay." I look at him as he stares out the window, perhaps considering whether the personal costs he had paid over the years were worth it for him.

"He might have nothing, too. But it can't hurt to help him by checking."

"Yeah, okay."

"He's gonna need a bit more help, you know," Bails said, getting to the larger point he was trying to make in almost in a whisper now. It was the sort of discussion we would often have back at work in more normal circumstances: sensitive information handed over to someone who could do something about it, without letting too many people know.

I encouraged him to share more. "How so?"

"He's still only so raw as a coach," Bails went on. "Think about it– he's been in only for two years. Pete Carroll had to go more than a decade before he became really good. Phil Jackson didn't take quite as long, but he didn't become a legend overnight. Even in AFL, Clarko and Bomber were both close to being sacked early on, but now look at them."

I nodded. I'd been thinking that myself recently, and the example he raised was especially relevant - the two AFL coaches he referred to by nickname had won five of the last seven titles between them, despite each starting their careers with a three or four inconsistent years. With the season so close, though, I wasn't quite sure what we could do from here in terms of extra support in Bails' absence.

"I think he knows that too," Bails suggested. One of my eyebrows raised its hand, but Bails didn't even wait for me to ask for an explanation to give one this time.

"He came round to my place the day he got the news about me," Bails coughed, and then continued. "I was sitting out on the balcony with the family, all pretty flat. Then the bell rings, and Caron goes to answer it.

"It was Sando, he came as soon as he heard. He didn't really know what to say– what can you say? But he did say, *'I can't do it without ya' mate.'* I think he worries how he'll go without the help, you know?"

167

I did, and it was something that those within the staff all knew but hadn't broached yet. Bails had been a great help for Sando in many areas, not the least of which was in keeping his workload down by sharing media and player management duties. But perhaps more importantly, he was a trusted, objective set of eyes to help Sando maintain a steady keel toward the bigger goal. Bails had once famously told Sando to *take a deep breath, you're just having a bad day, not a bad life*.

"Not sure if he was saying it to make me feel better." Bails attempted to play it down.

"Don't think so, mate," I cut him off. "I think we're all worried about that. It came up when we had the General in talking about resilience last week. All the coaches – especially Bicks, 'cos he loves that shit – were right into it. Sando at first was attentive and then seemed distracted, and I thought, 'Oh shit, he's just not into it.'

Bails cocked his head to the side, looking at me, curious to hear more.

"But in the end, it got to a conversation of 'Look, we've had some bad luck, it seems like we're a bit cursed'. These are Sando's words: *Feels like we just need to win, we need some positives*. And you can see where he's sort of leading it, and then he says *I don't know how I'm gonna handle what's coming up, with Bails' situation*.'"

It was something that had been troubling me in my down time, of which there was little. How do we even begin to handle something like this, and still go out and get things done once games come around? "We've already spoken about it from a welfare point of view for the group: if the worst-case scenario eventuates, here's what we'll do. But for the head coach..." I trailed off, because I didn't yet have an answer.

Tears welled up in Bails' eyes now, and he looked away from me and toward the wall. As the ultimate team man, it hurt him to be leaving his guys like this, unable to help. I left the conversation alone and let him process his thoughts until he felt comfortable to talk again. It wasn't long before he started fiddling with the TV remote - a sign I took to say he was okay to continue, but perhaps on another topic.

"Do you think much about when you played?" I asked, taking the talk to what should be happier thoughts.

"When I played?"

"As in nowadays," I tried to clarify, "do you think back to your playing days?"

"Um..." He looked down at his phone, which had begun to dance along the edge of the table. "Hang on, just text me wife."

"Go right ahead." Bails fumbled after his phone at first, either distracted by thoughts still lingering from the raw topic we just left or maybe just twitching while he reached for it. As soon as he had a good grip on it, he started tapping away.

He finished his text and set the phone down. "I think my wife's gonna be coming over, Paddy." Then, frowning, he asked, "What was the question?"

"Do you think much about playing?" I repeated.

"Oh. Nah, not really. Every now and then, but nowhere near as often as some people would think, but no."

"So it doesn't inform the way you coach?" I tried to rephrase it when he looked confused. "The experiences you had as a player, is that what you based your style on, maybe in the earlier years? Or after that, you saw coaches mostly, so you based your coaching on other coaches?"

He considered for a moment. "I based some of what I was doing on the coaches who coached me. And then reading about the coaches throughout the world, on how they – some of the tactics and techniques they use. I still watch the press conferences of some of the NFL guys, the English blokes in the premier league. You just pick up a few things – some of the shit the Yanks come up with is just beautiful." I chuckled, knowing we had laughed about this topic over our early breakfasts in 2011, when I had revealed how much I loved American sports.

"I heard Jimmy Mora, who coached the Atlanta Falcons, three years, maybe four years ago now. Jimmy said, after a reporter asked him, 'What are you gonna do now?'"

Bails clears his throat, and prepares his American accent. "He says, *'We're gonna evaluate every scheme. We're gonna evaluate every run. Then we'll evaluate every pass.'* And I thought, what a great answer. If I was a supporter sitting there going, 'This coach is gonna analyse every single part of the game'. I thought that was a pretty smart answer. Whether it was an audible at the line of scrimmage, whether it was coach's call, whether it was a run, a pass. Whatever it is, make sure it was the right call, and then make sure they were all on the same page. Hard to break down, 'cos it's just so correct and there's no obvious hole.'"

"So, I pick up things from other coaches," Bails nodded his head, "who goes off their tree and who doesn't. I think that's interesting, gives you an insight into their personality, I reckon. Plus I'd have chats with the other coaches, dissecting other coaches. I learn more from those talks than just by myself."

That reminded me of a problem back at the coalface. "Had a few guys come and complain this week, too, just about the program and how much is on – too much, according to some."

"Ah, okay." He nodded and wiped again at his mouth and chin. "Too hard for them?"

"It seems like that." For a moment I'm overcome with anger, thinking about all that the man in front of me is going through, while others complain that they are worked too hard. The feeling wasn't altogether foreign – I recognised it from another time I'd watched Bails suffer.

The first day of Bails' suspension in 2013 was like any other on the shop floor: players lifting, coaches cutting, trainers rubbing. For some though, the absence was palpable.

As we filed into the players room for the catered lunch, I flicked Bails a text:

U in ur new office at the moment chief?

His response seconds later suggested he had read my mind:

Yes in meeting room, waiting for lunch to be
delivered. or at least a crumb ???

I took a picture of the pasta meal I'd packed for him into a Tupperware container, and sent it through. Barely a moment had gone by for him to start salivating before his reply shot back.

Hurry up and deliver it.

I chuckled, and ambled back through the locker room, past the football reception area. It was cool compared to the March heat I walked out into, on my way across to the Admin building which he had been confined to as punishment for his still unspecified crime against sport.

Bails cut a lonely silhouette up in the meeting room, his new office for the next sixteeen weeks. I found him hunched over his laptop towards one end of the board room sized table where we would normally sit as a coaching staff to select the team each week. The sound of rustling foil and the door closing behind me lifted his head, but it was the scent of the pasta sauce that lifted the corners of his mouth.

"You sure know the way to a coach's heart, Paddy," he smirked as he closed his laptop. Business was on hold while he welcomed what would come to be a rare visitor from the football side.

"Can't stay long in case the fun police see it as a breach of the Geneva Convention," I joked. "Just wanted to see how things look here at your new workplace."

171

"It's not bad – think I'll do some review for Nobes on recruiting stuff, and maybe some coaches' box audio analysis. Can't directly work on anything football related though, so I'll be open to other projects. Triggy said he's got a couple of ideas."

As Bails looked out the window, a small group of players filed out for a touch session. His gaze held a moment longer than necessary, his mind contemplating what he now couldn't do. Teaching was his drug of choice. And now he had been put into an involuntary detox, with no methadone-like replacement to ease the cravings. Cold turkey was the order, served with a side of isolation.

"You're doing a perfect '*Good To Great*'," I tried to turn his focus away from what he was missing by aiming it towards something he loved, the classic book by Jim Collins. "Every group in that book who made the leap to being great, their management team responded to adversity with a balance: on one hand they faced the brutal facts of reality, while on the other hand they kept an optimistic outlook towards the end goal."

"Yeah," Bails took the ball I'd thrown him and ran with it. "You gotta confront reality. It's like a player who's been dropped, 'cos I can bitch and moan all I like, but it's not gonna change anything, is it?"

He had a point, and as always, a way of seeing things from a different angle.

"All I can do is take what I'm dealt, and think, 'This is how things are, so what can I do now?' It's not forever. No doubt I'll get into some good stuff at this end though. Nobes is at the real pointy end when it comes to analytics and setting up the metrics stuff."

We both looked around for something to take the weight out of the conversation. The food was as good a deflection as any.

"I presume Enzo is missing me already?"

I laughed, happy the topic was back to common interests rather than how disengaged he was about to be for the next few months. Enzo Fazzari was the chef of choice for the player and coach lunches, so of course Bails had gone out of his way to get on Enzo's good side.

"No doubt. I'll tell him you said hi when I get back there. Gotta run for now though, got meetings in five."

"Okay mate, good stuff."

I left Bails in purgatory and headed back to the real football world. As I was about to head into the next meeting, a text from Bails came through.

Thanks very nice, half today half tomorrow.
What can I say.

I tried to think of something to quickly write back, but I found nothing. The problem was, there was nothing I could say right at that moment. There weren't enough words to fill the waiting space that lay ahead for Bails.

Back in the setting of his latest limbo, Bails shifted on the pillow filled bed, adjust his nasal tubes again now more for habit than effect. He seemed less comfortable today than I had seen him since when he was adjusting every other minute on his makeshift bed at home. I offered to help him move.

"Nah Im good thanks Paddy." He replied with a listless gesture of the hand. "But everything's going well, though?"

"Yeah, touch wood." I lightly rapped my knuckles on the arm of my chair. "Apart from Ricky – you hear about that, did you?"

Ricky Henderson, a dynamic defender who had crossed over from basketball, had broken his leg in a tackling incident at training the day before. He would miss most of the season now as well.

"Yeah, that's shocking."

"It's terrible, and it's unexpected, but this is a contact game and it could've happened at any point. That's football. I was surprised by how quickly the tone around the place became so negative around everything. Particularly the coaches and players, some saying, *'We can't take a trick,' 'We're fucking unlucky,'* and, *'There's a frickin' curse on this place.'*"

"Oh, really?" he asked and then held the tissue over his mouth as he hocked up a loogey, a wet and uncomfortable sound.

"Which is interesting, given there's only a couple of injuries – well, and they're obviously referring to your situation, as well."

"Oh, yeah. Hm..." Bails looked down, unsure what to say to that.

"One of the good things that General Cornum left us with was a question. We didn't really answer it, but it's something I think is gonna be so useful, and we definitely need it. *Is this the worst thing that could happen?* The key guys in the group need to think about that, so they can be more comfortable dealing with reality, and also optimistic about pressing on. That helps when adversity comes up. You gotta be able to make sense of it in your own story. Like, *'Yep, this is shit, but it makes sense in the story I'm eventually gonna tell about my life.'*"

"Mm..., yeah."

"How are you goin' with that sort of stuff?" I transitioned from others hardships to his own. Like running from the soft sand straight into the ocean.

"Oh, I'm goin' okay." He didn't seem to be putting on a brave face any more, because his decline was becoming so obvious. "As well as I can. Every day I wake up, I'm happy. I'm in pain for the first couple of hours, last couple of days I've been a bit better..."

There came a rapid knock-knock on the door and a nurse – an Asian woman, dark hair pulled back from her face – poked her head in. "Can I come in?"

"Yeah," we both said in unison, although I was getting a bit frustrated. It always seemed like there was an interruption just when we got to the juicy stuff.

"Hi, Dean," she greeted him in accented English. "I just got call from radiotherapy. Your time is two sirty."

"Oh. Two thirty?"

She nodded, smiling as she helped him adjust his position. "Which is good, yes. So we do morphine 'bout two o'clock."

"Okay, great." Bails required a lot of help to move in bed now, so his gratitude was genuine towards the nurse who had just moved him. "Thanks."

"Is okay," she replied in accent again. "You want me help you with shower or anything?"

"No. I'm right. Thanks."

"Okay, I will come later. See you." She waved at Bails and headed back toward the door.

"Bye," we told her, again in unison, as she pulled the door shut again on her way out. When she was gone, Bails picked up where we'd left off.

"No, I know exactly where I am. It's hard, no one wants it, I don't want it. You can dwell on it, or you can keep thinking about all the shit that's gone on, or you can just try and enjoy as much of the day as you can. If I'm gonna go, how do I want to spend these days?"

He shifted on the bed, straightening his legs beneath the sheet. It reminded of his immobility.

"I struggle to move around now," he lamented. "My legs are wasting away."

Renowned for his stocky legs, with calves that you couldn't pull socks over, it was obvious to anyone who knew him that his legs had indeed begun to shrink in size.

"Your calves are still bigger than my chicken legs!" I tried a joke to buoy his spirits.

"Ha." He snorted. "Before I could walk the wards. So I've gotta try and get back to walking the wards. If I could do it a week ago, ten days ago, I should be able to do it tomorrow, or if not tomorrow, the next day, or the next day. Just keep moving forward. Inch by inch, didn't Al Pacino say *In Any Given Sunday*?"

It was a classic movie, a piece we had recited from time to time. His voice reminded me of Pacino's these days, hoarse and damaged, but full of spirit.

"Just put a few little goals, timelines in place. I wanna be there at Adelaide Oval, for the first game, uh... March 29? I wanna see the stadium lit up, night game. That's gonna be fantastic. Little things like that I'm just trying to focus on – don't think too far past that if I can."

For a moment there is more breath in his lungs, a little more life in his eyes. I smile. "Sounds like the old 'contest by contest' line."

He laughed. "Yeah, one contest at a time."

"Makes me think of Victor Frankl," I offered, searching my memory for the actual quote I wanted to give him. "The guy who survived the Nazi camps in the war – he said something like, *'Those who have a* why *to live for can push through almost any* how.'"

"Hm." Bails sat still for a moment, staring out the window. He looked to be considering the similarities in their situations for a moment, or perhaps he was just picturing the goals in his head. "One step at a time. Who knows? The chemo..."

He hesitated, a combination of determination and frustration in his voice. "The radiation helped last time I had it, but its spreading through me, I can feel it. It's not as if I can ignore that." He grimaced. "So, BP is okay, the oxygen saturation is still okay, some of those indicators are still acceptable. Couple of the cancer lymphs are growing; where ten days ago they seemed to be okay, now they're growing again. I had three weeks of basically nothing, you know, so you'd expect something to fight back. So..."

The talk of the losing battle seemed to visibly change his energy, pulling him down into dark depths. I tried to drag us back ashore.

"You getting much time to yourself," I ask, "or you getting a heap of visitors and a heap of treatment and stuff to keep you busy?"

"Yeah, visitors come and go."

"So there's not a lot of time to sit and think?"

"Oh, no, there's plenty of time to sit and think," he said with a heavy dose of regret. "Too much. But I get visitors coming all sorts of times. That's a pain in the ass sometimes, but it's a good thing most of the time. But I'd much rather when visitors come in, they tell me about what they're doing at work rather than talk about what's happening in this four walls... wash basin... prison bed." Although I knew he was dead serious about the frustration of everyone wanting to talk about him and what he was going through, there was a sly look on his face.

"That a sneaky Cold Chisel reference?" I asked, eyes narrowed in mock suspicion.

"Yeah." A small grin. A small win.

"Nice." I nodded my approval.

He took his own advice and turned the conversation back to something he longed for: the coaching life. "Dave Mackay must've played all right on the weekend?"

"Campo said it's the best he's seen him play," I confirmed. I thought the same.

"That's good."

"Think I said last time, his training is as good as I've seen – he's been sharp, his patterns are spot on, he's moving through contests at top gear. And he's out of his shell a little, too. And I don't expect that will change anytime soon, either. Yeah, he's going well."

"I might just send him a text. Climb back into his head again." He gave a wry grin, then cleared his throat, hocking up another huge loogey. "Well, that's good." He spat into the crumple of tissues still in his hand. "And Mitch Bailey?"

I smiled. "Mitch Bailey is IN. He's locked in. He came in yesterday to meet with me, and I was stuck in a meeting so I was two minutes late. By the time I got out the front to meet him, he was already talking to Sloaney, and Dougy says, 'G'day', so all the boys are around him."

"Yeah, Darcy says the same thing when he's in for State League training. He says, 'It's nice they know my name.' It's good that they can say hello to him. Use the first name, carries a bit of weight..."

"It's funny, they call Darcy 'Darc', but they call Mitch 'Bails.'"

"Oh, do they? Ha." He smiled to himself, pleased.

"Ooo...," I interrupted the conversational flow, "just found a cheeky marshmallow in the top of my drink."

"Oh, you lucky prick," he chuckled before getting us back on track. "How's Danger going with his captaincy?"

I laugh at the sarcasm. Even though he and Sloane had been appointed joint vice captains, after an injured skipper and a media frenzy some had taken it upon themselves to anoint Danger as the lone captain now. "Yeah, okay. Not much to do just yet. I don't expect either of them to change a heap in the first half of the year. With the added pressure, they're more likely to revert back to their norms, rather than change anything. But they'll both love it, I haven't seen any trepidation."

"They wouldn't have had to do a lot yet, yeah?"

"Yeah. And they won't – yeah, we still have VB there, we still point media to him, he's still in the strategy meetings. If there's any behaviour issues, VB's still the one who stamps his feet. Or one foot and one moon-boot."

"Yeah, gotta be careful with that Achilles."

178

We stopped talking for a bit, him to catch his breath again, and me to finish my hot chocolate. While I drank, I thought about Sando and all Bails could teach him, if he only had the time.

"What advice would you give Sando?" I asked when the silence felt too long. "You might have been able to give it to him direct, but..."

I leaned back in my chair, sensing where we were headed. I'd started the topic without much thought, hopeful he'd give me something simple I could take back to Sando the next day. Now the conversation hung in the air, silent and still as a frosted football field on a winter's morning. The pause almost taunted us, asking if we really wanted to tackle the elephant in the room. I had an idea.

"I guess you had to deal with similar things in the same seat," I suggest, "when you had to deal with the job while Jimmy Stynes was struggling with cancer." Despite the acrimony of his ending at Melbourne, Bails had always spoken highly of Jim as a person. He knew better than anyone the effect that ordeal had on the club, coaches, and players. "What sort of advice would you give to Sando to be able to handle... that?"

Bails was silent. He contemplated not only his looming destiny but at the same time relived a tough time from his own coaching experience. This was the first time we had truly broached the inevitability of what was coming, and I wasn't sure how uncomfortable it might be. I needn't have worried, because once he had cleared the mucus from his throat, the wisdom poured out.

"If there's one thing I know about that position," Bails rasped, "it's to expect the unexpected. I mean, he already knows that from all the shit that's happened since he arrived."

To say Sando had been unlucky as a senior coach would be an understatement. In the two seasons since he had taken the coveted role, his team had been fined, lost draft picks, and had the CEO and GM of football suspended. If that off-field distraction wasn't enough, his senior assistant coach was suspended, his budding superstar struck down with an ACL, and his captain lost for a season. Now his friend and mentor was stricken with an incurable cancer. All of it was out of his control, and some even came as ripple effects from events in the past and at other clubs.

"The biggest thing is to know that you can't control everything - even when you're at the top - and that all you can do is make the most of whatever you're dealt. Keep your eyes up on the bigger picture, remember why you're there, and you'll be okay."

The profound simplicity of this statement seemed to mute the whole floor. No nurses or bedpans rattled in the background now, as if the whole hospital had paused to listen to Bails dispense his wisdom.

"Everything will come to an end – your career as a player, your job as a coach."

Your time on earth, I thought. I kept that to myself.

"And when you think that's too hard, you can always look back at other times and find some that were just as hard. Or if you think about it hard enough, it could be worse. Doesn't mean it's easy, but you know it isn't the end of the world..."

A strong coughing fit took over Bails now, and he reached for tissues. After he had expelled the crap from his mouth, he tried to sum it up in relation to how we got started on the topic.

"So for what's coming up, the thing he's gotta remember," Bails fought a cough, "always gotta remember," another cough, "is that you'll always get through."

More coughs, as I sat there and absorbed what Bails had just said. The hospital seemed to come alive again with a clatter in the hallway, and combined with Bails' next wave of coughs, this was enough to suggest the magic was over for today.

"Mate, I really appreciate all of this," I said as I reached to gather my things. "I don't wanna wear you out though."

When he had regained his breath again, Bails just nodded and said, "No worries." He was ready for a rest.

"I'll see you again soon, mate."

"Sure will," he rasped. "Look forward to it."

SESSION 8 – DRIVE

| | | |

The stunned silence in the locker room spoke even louder than the boos that the team had received only moments earlier as they walked off AAMI Stadium.

The great form that led to a pre-season cup only a month or two ago now seemed so far away. The first two games had been a breeze, and the reality check a week ago was simply a hiccup. Going into this game against one of the league's new expansion teams, most expected the Crows to waltz in at home.

Not so fast.

As the players had looked up at the scoreboard on their way off at the halftime break, the numbers showed the team leading only by 2 straight shots. Now the tension in the locker room was palpable. The shock stood out on the players' faces players like beads of sweat. Even the most experienced seemed unsure about how to set things right.

Sando had made quick time across the field, not far behind his players; there was lots to fix. His frustration was boiling after sitting in the coach's box for the past hour of below-average football. Reaching the room shortly after, they sit down at their lockers and he let the players know in no uncertain terms what he thought.

"That's just shit!" He screamed at them. He walked around the corner to begin the debrief with his assistant coaches, then had second thoughts and stuck his head back into the room where the players slumped.

"You're an embarrassment!" He concluded with a pointing finger, slamming the door shut behind him as he left the players to themselves.

Aside from the team doctor talking in hushed tones with each player to check for injuries or niggles, there was silence. The group seemed frozen, unsure how to handle the first negative emotions since the new coaching staff had moved in.

Bails walked into the locker room a few seconds after Sando exited.

"You know what you gotta do?" he asked no one in particular, and yet everyone at the same time.

Some players looked up, desperate for an answer, or even the directions to where they might find one. Others kept their heads down, fearful of another blast. Those who did look up saw him extend his arms by his side and flap them in small waves.

"Just shake it out." The players who did see him didn't know what to do – some smiled, others breathed out. A couple more looked up.

"Just shaaaake it out. Let it all go. Just shaaaake it out."

Like an enthusiastic Broadway singer holding the last note of her performance, Bails shakes his hands and arms with vigor. He has control of every pair of eyes in the room now and, by association, their lungs as well. Breathing settles, positive chatter begins, and the air that was so tense only minutes before was normal again.

As they regained their composure, and the players' talk picked up again, he moved into the meeting room where he sidled up to Sando. The club had brought Bails in to help guide the rookie senior coach and potentially be the release valve when the pressure went up. In hushed tones, he walks through a couple of simple strategy suggestions, mixed in with tips the coach can try to ensure the troops are relaxed but refocused. Sando becomes visibly calmer before his halftime address.

With team and coach reset, the Crows go on to deal with the younger, lighter opponent as they should. Confidence is restored, and in the weeks that follow, the team nets a series of big scalps that weren't expected. All the while they played the loose, instinctive brand of football that Sando, Bails, and the other coaches encourage.

And by the end of that year, heading into finals, the team that had finished fourteenth the previous year was tied for first place.

SESSION 8
DRIVE
WE TALK ABOUT CULTURE & MOTIVATION

"As this gets tougher, what can the rest of us do to help?"

Bails opened his mouth to answer but that just dissolved into a cough. When it had passed, he said, "Good question, Paddy. Ah..."

His voice was now as raspy as I'd ever heard it, and there was a constant wheeze as he took most breaths. His words were slow to come out and required an extra keen ear to decipher at times thanks to his tongue swelling in response to the medication. Barely any time had passed since our last session, and yet he seemed to have aged ten years.

"Probably text a couple of times during the week – that's all. Because I can't talk a lot – or I choose not to talk a lot – um, probably the best thing to do is drop a couple of texts during the week."

He took a short sip of water, then spat into the bag by his bed. There was no chance for anything that he sipped to make its way into his stomach.

"Um," he pressed on, "if anything happens at training that's notable, or anything in the game that's worth noting, and also... throw a couple of projects at me. Where you say, *'continue to do what you've been doing before with the analysis of the game and everything, and we'll work out a way to get your laptop to you'.*"

I cringed inside, but kept a poker face up for Bails. With where he found himself now, the extent of the disease, and the need for lightning fast turnarounds on video edits, his suggestion was more of a daydream than a possibility.

"Um," he kept on, even if he did know it was futile. "I'd make sure I've got a few games to watch every week, and watch the trends of the game – wouldn't be any more than that. Text a couple of times during the week, and probably one call a week. Only needs to be five minutes – these aren't deep and meaningful, half-an-hour discussions. Might be just ten-fifteen minutes, you talk about the game or talk about something separate."

I wondered if he had momentarily forgotten the king sized elephant that was wedged here in the back corner of room 440.

"I know what's going on inside me," he rasped, as if reading my mind. As he coughed again, I breathed a sigh of relief knowing that we wouldn't have to tiptoe around the obvious. "That's why I don't need to repeat it to everyone. But if I had a couple of games to code, to analyse, to look at, then that'll give me something to do in the sense of..."

He paused, searching for the right words.

"Feeling like I'm still helping in some sense."

"That's a good point." I could tell just by the way he spoke, rambling, searching, that one of his biggest discomforts right now was not feeling like he was of any use to the team. He had invested so much into football, and indeed our team, it seemed impossible for him to let go.

"That'd be about all, wouldn't need any more than that. If you've got the time, probably drop in once a week, and if Sando wants he can just drop the drive off or the computer off. Or he can pick it up, or Darcy can take it into work. That's not an issue." His voice trailed off, and he plucked at the sheets on the bed, frustration as he thought about all the things he couldn't do.

"Okay. Are you comfy?" I asked, moving to more immediate matters that I could actually help with. The grunt was dismissive.

"Are you okay with me asking you stuff that's about what you're going through and about how you're feeling?"

185

"Oh," he swallowed, then coughed, "yeah, some of it I am, some of it..." Coughing again. "If I'm not, I just won't answer."

"Okay. Good." I paused for a moment, getting myself settled and checking the phone was recording. "This is a football thing. I wanna know what advice you'd give to someone who..." No, that wasn't the right intro, not for what I wanted. I started over again. "How old were you when you started coaching?"

"Ah..." He smiled a little, drifting back into memories. "Mt. Gravatt, '96, I think. Ninety-four, '95..." He tapped his fingers on the mattress as he did the math in his head. "Ninety-six, I think. Born in '67. So 29."

I nodded. "So someone like Heath or myself, who are at the start of a coaching career. If you could go back then, and were at the start, what advice would you give? Having gone through what you've gone through since '96, what would your pearl of wisdom be? Or pearls, plural?"

"Hah!" He huffed in place of a laugh, all he could manage around a cough. "Oh, everyone's path's a bit different. Mine was a bit different, 'cos I'd work during the day. I had an export job so I travelled overseas every two weeks. So for two weeks I'd be home, and then for two weeks I'd be away from my wife and kids. I'd fly back into Australia and go straight to training, even though I'd been away from the family for so long."

That was poles apart from today's industry, where coaching holds the potential to be a legitimate, full-time job for someone stepping straight out of the game if they wanted.

"What I found beneficial was having to deal with all the little shitty jobs, when I was a senior coach, because I had to learn on my own how to coach my own team. All the little shitty things."

"That was beneficial?" I mentally thumbed through a couple of things that an old coach could consider "shitty" jobs.

"Oh, yeah. They were beneficial. You know, contracts, sitting in a change room talking about ten or fifteen dollars more. It seemed petty to me, but it wasn't about the money. It was more the principle of it all: 'I know you're worth more, we'd love to pay you more, but we can't.'" I did know. That sort of thing is almost a universal constant. "And then trying to find resolutions to it."

"Can you give us an example?" I probed for more detail, fascinated by this flashback. Bails was happy to indulge.

"Dealing with guys who couldn't train during the week. There was a plumber who was down on the Gold Coast doing his apprenticeship during the week, and then he'd play for us on the weekends. So he might have done twelve or fifteen sessions pre-season, didn't train at all during the season."

He paused for a sip of water, hands trembling, then continued.

"Now he isn't one of your highest paid players thanks to that, but he IS one of your better players. He just is. You gotta deal with that. You just gotta deal with shit."

His gaze roamed the room, lighting here and there as he thought, remembered. I stayed quiet, not wanting to interrupt his flow.

"The club went into bankruptcy," he began again, lighting on a key memory. "Couldn't pay anyone. Couldn't pay wages, couldn't pay salary, couldn't pay matches. And the president came to me and said, *'Look, our bank account's gonna be empty after this weekend, so we can't pay the players.'"*

"Wow." It wasn't the only time I'd heard such a story. What I wanted to hear more was how Bails handled it.

"He's told me this during the week, and I said we've gotta pull the players together and tell them, you can't just – you can't screw 'em round. And he said, *'Yeah, you're right. Can you deal with that?'* The guys on the board are saying the same thing, so I'm like, 'All right.'"

I watched him as he spoke. He looked tired, but even though he told me he wasn't talking much, he seemed more animated just then than he had in days, maybe weeks.

"So just before we went in there, in our changing rooms, there was two exit doors – one was to the left of me, and there was one down the back. I made sure the exit door down the back was locked. So the only way they could get out was to physically walk out past me to go through the exit door."

As he continued to speak, his voice got rougher, thicker. Finally he hocked up a loogey and spat into a wad of tissues.

"So," he continued, "I sat up there and told the players, 'Look guys, I've got some bad news. Club hasn't got any money. No one gets paid. I don't get paid, you don't get paid. After this Saturday, no one's getting paid.' And they said, 'Oh, right,' a few murmurs. I said, 'The reason I'm telling you now is you've still got two days before you can put your transfer in. It'd be unfair of me not to. It would be unfair if I told you Friday night and then you're pissed off 'cos you've got no transfer window.' And they said, 'Yep, we would've been, but at least you were honest and told us.'"

I had to laugh at that, just imagining the scene.

"And I said, 'There's only one thing though, boys. If you're gonna walk out on us and leave, you're gonna have to walk out in front of your mates. You're gonna have to stand up and leave through this exit door here – make it very clear that you're not coming back.' So I waited and waited. There were a few fidgety feet, but no one walked out, and I didn't think there would be. There might've been a couple who were thinking money wise, who mighta thought, 'Shit, there goes that $250 a week.' But everyone stayed."

We had gone over so much over our visits to this point, and yet this story still astounded me. Before me sat an encyclopedia of knowledge on not just our game, but on handling people, groups and communities. His now frail appearance belied the power of his wisdom.

"So that tests your ability to think on your feet," Bails went on. "You gotta try to still maintain your integrity and your honesty, but you also still gotta try and get everyone to stay, even against their best interests. 'Cos, you know, you can play for years and years and years, but you don't really play for the money – you play for the love of it, when it comes down to it. No one really thinks, 'I'm playing for money,' do they?"

"Not at that level, I wouldn't think." My statement buys time for Bails while he takes another sip of water. Voices out in the hall, indistinct through the closed door, grew louder but not clearer before fading away as the speakers passed. They were a reminder that we were in a hospital, not the musty wooden clubhouse of the local team.

"So those sort of things give you challenges from a senior coach's point of view – players not happy that they're not being picked: Why aren't I playing? I'm better than him. Why am I dropped? It's just crap. You get to face those sort of things early. Then I'd go to the development coaching role, where you're not involved in the hiring and firing as much. More involved in the skill aspect of it, the decision-making element, all that sort of stuff which I quite liked."

The only sounds in the room were the faint hum of the overhead lights, Bails' voice, and the occasional scratch as I checked my phone was getting all this.

"I had two years at Essendon," he said, "and then I went to a club like Port Adelaide, which was a natural progression, but they had really good IP. I think they were way ahead of every other team in regards to use of coding, use of technology. They were miles ahead, but I think they just lost that a little bit. 'Cos when personnel goes, and you don't get that group discussion on where you can take it, you lose that point of difference, I suppose. You become normal again."

"Yeah." Nodding my agreement, I took a swig from my water bottle.

"And then obviously on to Melbourne after that. The most important aspect is dealing with the unexpected as I mentioned –

and getting to know the players. If the player knows that you care for him, like, that you seriously wanna help him to be the best he can be, and the player believes that, then you're halfway there. Caring for the players is one thing – the player wants to know that – but, you know, they also need to be confident that you have the knowledge and skills to get them there. So there are a lot of other techniques coaches use to push them along and prod them at different times."

"Mm." I glanced down at my notes. "If you were starting at your pro career again – so when you arrived at Essendon – would you do anything differently?"

"Would I do anything differently at Essendon?"

"Or anywhere else in your whole professional coaching career?"

"Well, one good thing I did when I got to Essendon, I got them to pay for the level-three course for me. But that's probably the thing I regret a bit... I could've done a little bit more study into the psychology stuff then. I would've much preferred to have done a couple more years of the psychology stuff and then go as an assistant coaching. That would've set me up pretty well, I think, not just from a skills point of view, but would've also made me a bit different to everybody else. Yeah, probably just educational stuff really."

"In the flags you've coached in," I inquired, "is there a discernible difference in the attitude of a premiership team versus just any team? Melbourne when you were coaching, versus Port when you won a flag? What's the difference in mindset?"

"Melbourne had no belief. The belief that Essendon had... I went to Essendon in 2000 just as a development coach, walked in off the street. They were driven by that loss, the Carlton loss, so that was more of a massive motivation to prove that wrong."

"That was the year of the record?"

"Two thousand was the record year; they lost one game. The thing I found interesting there, Paddy, looking back on that, is the fact that they put a lot of it back on that loss, that prelim loss to Carlton. Maybe that's why they only won one."

He started letting his eyes wander around the room again, taking a visual walk while his body couldn't.

"Maybe when that drive and the motivation was gone, they were done. In 2001 they got beaten by Brisbane in the Grand Final, and that was it. Next time they got anywhere near it was... finals was a good four or five years later."

His eyes moved now from the window to the other visitors chair.

"But I think the motivation that drove them was the short-term embarrassment of the loss to Carlton. Once they won the Grand Final, it almost repaid it, you know what I mean? That was the drive, and now it's gone, it's disappeared." Eyes moved from the chair back to the window, as if he were pacing the room, giving a pre-game speech.

"Whereas at Port, they were a great team. The Bombers were a great team, but only won one, should've won two. Port was always striving towards it – they got knocked back: prelim loss, prelim loss, prelim loss, then prelim win. Then won the Grand Final. Going into the Grand Final against Brisbane, their game was good, but they were just dropping off a bit. They'd had a few injuries, and we wanted to win."

Window to chair.

"Win the Grand Final. Not because we'd lost the prelim the year before. Because it happened three years in a row, it took a lot of mental strength to get off the canvas and fight again and win. Once that was done it was *sky's the limit*'!"

He took a breath here. Only now did he notice how far into "coach mode" he had drifted - as much as his condition would allow - while he described some of the best days of his coaching career. He settled back into his supported sitting position now, and settled his voice at the same time.

"So the Port team was pretty tough," he continued. "Both teams were mentally tough; Essendon was super tough, but I think the Carlton loss fuelled the Essendon one. The Port one though... We knew if we could actually get through the prelim, we'd win."

The room fell quiet, and rather than insert another question I allowed him the moment to bask in the memories. The far-off look in his eyes now provided a glimpse into the other part of coaching that he loved as much as mentoring young men: Bails loved to compete. And to win.

"I remember walking to the Brisbane game," Bails continued after a brief lull. "There were a few Brisbane people there. I'm saying *'How you going?'* to them, and they make some smart-ass remark about history 'cos they were going for their fourth in a row. And to the Port people, and I said *'whattaya think?'* And they said *'oh, everyone reckons they're coming to watch history today.'* 'Yeah, they are, aren't they?' I said."

He turned over his shoulder to re-enact the moment. "'History here today is we're gonna win our first premiership, aren't we?' So people are here coming to see their fourth; no one's coming to see our first – even if you were neutral." His words confirmed what his face showed: he was no longer in the room, but rather right back outside the stadium on the biggest day of the season, reliving the day that all coaches dreamed about.

"But no," he said, glancing back over at me after basking in the victory for a few more moments, "the mental part of the game was huge. For Port to keep getting up three years in a row, it's impressive. We were good enough to win two premierships."

"So why didn't you win two?" I asked.

"Oh, we'd fail when it came to the first final. So we were weak in the first final, which meant we were up against it once we lost our advantage."

"It was the Magpies one year, wasn't it?" I recalled that game because my older brother, Carl, had been one of the conquering invaders from Collingwood.

"Yeah, Collingwood beat us, Sydney beat us, Hawthorn beat us. We lost our first finals; there was just such a build up of anxiety, pressure, it was just enormous after they got beaten by Hawthorn. So that just played on their mind, and they were always reminded of it. All pre-season, constant reminders: 'You're just throwing premierships away.' 'Port Adelaide doesn't do that.' And when you go there, you buy into that mindset."

His line about one of the strongest team identities in the history of Australian Football stirred another memory – this one in the heady days of the 2012 season, as we sat on top of the table in our first season, riding the wave of a rejuvenated team identity.

"Who do you like, Paddy?" the baseball was the focus of the SportsCenter broadcast on the screen in the video room of the club.

At the Crows, this room not only served as the cutting room for all of the edits and analysis, but also the coaches' version of the office water cooler. Small groups would often gather to talk about the rest of the sports world thanks to the big screen TV on the back wall, and sometimes the talk would turn to internal politics too.

"Giants," I replied, for the most part because I had just visited San Francisco that past off-season. "You?"

"Don't really follow it, to be honest." Bails was matter of fact.

"Yeah me neither," I fessed up. "I do like the Giants though, from what I know – looks like they are building a dynasty right now, and they aren't buying it like they normally do in baseball."

"Like a Moneyball thing?" Bails asked, referring to the no famous story of the Oakland A's Billy Beane.

"Nah, its even better," I replied. "It's culture."

"How do you know that?"

"They've gone against the popular recipe," I explained. "Traditionally in baseball the higher the payroll, the higher the chance of winning. But you *can* measure money spent against ROI. The Giants ranked #10 in payroll for 2010, when they won. And it hasn't changed much this year."

Bails sipped his coffee, eyes on the screen as plays of the day flicked through, but nodded to show he was listening.

"So how do you know it's their culture?" he probed.

"Well," I expanded, "even on the Moneyball stats this thing they use to measure talent - Wins Above Replacement - they weren't the best either. The thing that stands out is they let the players have some autonomy, which is rare in the richest team sports."

"Like the Leading Teams thing at Geelong and Hawthorn?" Bails looked at me to gauge a visual reaction before I could answer. He knew I had worked with Ray McLean's well-known company as a facilitator of leadership programs, and was testing my view. "People always talk about how they gave them power and that was what made them blossom. Didn't work that well for us at Melbourne. Our players – hell, our club – they weren't ready."

"Hmm," I replied, thinking to myself that the surrounding instability at the club level, and the lack of trust that caused, was probably more to blame than his players' readiness. "Well, even if you ignore those teams' results, there's data in the military, healthcare, Google even, which shows that with the right balance of autonomy from the top down, people develop a different type of motivation that makes them persist longer. So if you let people choose to buy into it, they go a little further for the group."

194

"Sounds like Lombardi," Bails chimed in, referring to a biography on the legendary coach that I knew he had been devouring that month. "Something like '*Those with the most invested are the last to surrender*'"

I laughed, and nodded – this was a favourite quote of Ray's, which I had heard many times.

Bails turned back to the TV, not dismissing the idea, but not conceding either. Ironically, these open debates that Bails loved and encouraged were a perfect example of the type of leadership that builds the cultures we were talking about.

Without knowing it, Bails led his teams there naturally.

As the break in conversation that filled room 440 stretched out, Bails' eyes started to roll back in his head. His breathing became short, staccato almost, as if he needed to cough but couldn't.

"How you traveling, mate?" I asked, concerned. "Breath all right? You okay?"

There was no response at first, and then slowly his eyes gained focus again, and he lifted his head. A strong cough allowed him to talk again.

"Yeah, I'm okay, mate." He shook his head and shoulders then, like a dog, but not as hard. "I don't get a lot of sleep, so sometimes I'll just drift off if my body feels like it."

"If I'm asking you questions and you're struggling to breathe and stuff..." The last thing I wanted was to make him worse.

"No way." He waved off my concerns with a flap of his wrinkled, pale hand. "I'm breathing okay."

To give him a little more time to recover, I drank some water and flipped through some notes on my phone. When he seemed to be getting restless, I asked, "What's next in the game?"

His eyes narrowed, like an artist looking at a canvas. Bails was known as a keen thinker in the game, and he didn't disappoint here, setting off on a tour of his thoughts about the game: how the admin will be structured; what the head coach will look like; integrating departments like medical and strength; changing the physical layout of the coach and staff workspaces; the new space at Adelaide Oval, and what it will do for the game, on and off the field.

After a bit, he turned back to me. "What else you wanna talk about?"

He almost seemed urgent to push on, take everything that was on the menu like he used to when his appetite was strong. Maybe he sensed we might not get many more opportunities to get his thoughts down.

"The shit that you went through over the last few years, starting at Melbourne, and then being dragged into Adelaide. I know I spoke to you a few times once you were here, about the stuff that was going on, and then the suspension and that." I wasn't sure how I wanted to phrase it.

"Talking about meaning before: how did you come to terms with all that? Besides going, 'You assholes' and all that. How did you make sense of it? Or take positives out of it?"

"How did I handle that period?"

I nodded. "The general talked about 'post-traumatic growth' in the army, instead of – well, everyone's heard of post traumatic stress..."

"Yeah."

"But they've actually found evidence that some people can go through shit, and they take stuff out of it that's positive for them as a person."

"Oh," Bails acknowledged the idea, but moved to explain how he'd handled it rather than whether he grew. "One of the things I think I do well is I can park a problem and leave it there and not get flustered by it. Leave it there until I come up with a...

196

a better solution than what I've already put next to it. I try and prioritize a little better when I'm under that sort of stress." He nodded while he spoke. "So when I was under that sort of stress – and I've got no doubt that the stress certainly has had an impact on..."

Pausing for another moment, he tapped his fingers on the bed while he decided what to say.

"One of the things that bring the cancer on is high-stress levels." He nodded again, now reaching up under his arm, where he was noticeably thicker than the rest of his withering frame. His pursed lips suggested that, just for a moment, he was thinking of those who had given him the most stress. "Yeah, I think I was able to just put it into some sort of sequence, like, 'Don't worry about that yet, just think about this.' I tried not to worry about the upcoming six months down the track."

He focused on me again, his hand going still. "Which most people would. Just deal with this part of the issue first and try and solve it. So I think I did that part pretty well.

"When I went interstate, I'd go to the footy and people would recognize me. Pretty soon I decided I wasn't gonna have my hoodie on trying to hide. I decided there was no point in doing that. I used to have a hoodie, but I'd take the hood off, drop it off, and just go to the places I wanted to go. I'd go to the same coffee spots I wanted to go, stand behind someone in the line, and just do what I would normally do and what I wanted to do. I said to Caron when I got the news, 'There's no bloody way I'm gonna hide.'"

"Might as well take the whole thing head on, in one sense. 'Cos I've got nothing to hide, in a sense. Most people, when they run into me, a couple would have a crack at me but just jokingly. Like 'Ha ha ha, yeah, funny joke, dickhead.' But I didn't have a lot of them. I had more people, you know, 'It's great that you were able to put forward your side of the story,' they'd say."

My laughter that time had an ironic edge – I knew from previous discussions he had never had a chance to tell the full story. He still hadn't. Not to the rest of the world.

"The public reaction was quite good – not sure if it was 'cos they didn't wanna upset me, or they thought, 'He's been through a shitload already.'"

He picked up his phone, lips still pursed as if focusing on the sources of his stress. It was only a slight surprise that he turned to an old nemesis.

"So Mark Robinson's on the phone – on my phone – now, today, 'Oh, Dean, can you please give me a ring?'"

"What for?" I asked.

"Well, 'cos I've got cancer, and it's a story. Why else would he be ringing me?"

"He's gotta be fucking kidding!" I practically shouted, outraged given what I knew he had written about Bails while he coached at Melbourne.

"Mm. They're amazing people; if I'd written an article about Dean Bailey, and I'd written 'Dead Man Walking,' I'd be expecting a real big serve if I rang up! Like we're best buddies. Timmy Watson has been ringing me for a while – he rung me on about four occasions, 'Just seeing how you're going with everything.'"

A hoarse cough snuck up on Bails. "He's okay." He tried to talk through it. "Nah, I get along well with Tim. What else?"

"Ah, what else was I gonna say before?" I rifled through topics in my head before I finally remembered. "Oh, there's a couple of things: politics, or culture. Which one is more important to a premiership?"

"Politics? Jesus." He shook his head, then paused to think about how to word his response. "Culture. You can have politics in an organisation that may not be great, but it doesn't affect the players. The culture affects everyone though. Yeah, culture." He coughed into the crook of his elbow. "How you get them to buy into most things."

His answer was what I expected, and led perfectly to my next question.

"You had Jimmy Plunkett come to Melbourne, yeah?" I had grown up in the football world at the same time as Jimmy. We represented our state team at the National Championships together, were drafted the same year, and eventually found our way to working at the same company. Leading Teams was synonymous with discussions of culture in the AFL, having helped engineer the three most dominant teams - Geelong, Hawthorn and Sydney - in the last decade. "So you've seen the Leading Teams model, versus the in-house, versus nothing."

"Yeah," Bails concurred.

"Is it something that's reliant on the program, or the facilitator, or just if you have the right people at the time? Or is it that if you have the right people, you don't need the program?"

He searched for the best way to answer for a second, and settled on the beginning as the best place to start.

"I was a bit sceptical when Jimmy came and said, *'It's best if I'm part time, and that I'm not with the team full time.'* I asked him, 'Wouldn't you wanna see the regular stuff here?' And he said, *'Nah, I think it's better that I come in and out, 'cos if I'm here too often, there's that familiarity, you know.'* And so I said okay.'"

He paused, looking like he was readying himself for yet another coughing fit. It never arrived, and he continued.

"It's easy just to drift a little bit: one session can roll into another session. You don't get the benefit from it, you know. So the facilitator is super important. They've gotta win the trust of the group early. And they've gotta win the trust that what they're doing might actually work. And then they'll buy in, and ask questions. Once they buy in, you're flying. The group drives itself, it really comes from inside."

I nod, having seen it with my own eyes only a year earlier. "It's like the culture becomes the coach when the coach isn't there," I try to sum up what he has just said.

"Yep," Bails concurred, "that's what you see in the best groups. And as coach, you have to hand it over a little, because you want the players to do that too – give their own agenda up for the team. It can't be about you."

He paused, his voice trailing off. This team-first attitude was so Bails – both in football, and in life. It was one of the reasons he had first dug into the book collection in my office, picking up Phil Jackson's classic *Sacred Hoops*. Whilst coaching one of the greatest teams – and most talented individuals – in the history of basketball, Jackson had managed to build a culture at the Chicago Bulls that embodied what Bails thought was vital. As Jackson put it, players must *"sacrifice the 'me' in service of the 'we.'"*

I nodded, and then Bails coughed hard again. When his breathing returned, he seemed more drained than I had been aware of. "Anything else?" he asked hoarsely.

"Nah, I think we're out of conversation starters for the day!" I joked, picking up my phone & stopping today's recording. "Next time I'm coming in, I'll text you some topics in advance that you can pick from."

"Nah," Bails said, "you just choose."

"You handing the reins over?" I teased, playing on the theme of the visit and using his words.

"Ha." He huffed, then coughed again. Once he was under control again, he didn't answer with words, but instead gave me a knowing smirk. "See 'ya next time Paddy."

| | | |

113 *days.*

That's how long Bails had been without his drug of choice.

From the first Monday of the regular season, Bails had been on "suspension," denied the privilege of conversing with the players or coaches about football at all.

It began on March 18. Week 17 was an eternity away then, but on the first Tuesday of that week, the locker room was abuzz. Everyone was excited this week and rapt that he was back. Smiles. Hugs. Sarcastic jokes to play down the emotion. And around lunchtime, the playing group filed in for the first "Bails Strategy Meeting" in eighteen weeks.

"Now, I've been away for a bit, obviously, and some of you are no doubt wondering what I've been up to for my sixteen weeks of suspension. So I put together a little slideshow for you. Hit it, Brocky."

The lights went off. Brock Wiseman, one of the IT guys who'd helped put the upcoming show together, hit a switch and the projector hummed. Bails sat down. Only those close enough could see the early signs of a huge grin that began to grow on his face as the show started.

The next five minutes have been widely described by those who took part in it as perhaps the best memory of all their time with Bails.

It began with a still of Bails from a press conference, deep in thought. A cartoon thought bubble hinted at what was to come: "Hm... What should I do with sixteen weeks away from the club?"

And then, with Benny Hill's music kicking as the soundtrack, a series of images with the head of Dean Bailey superimposed came up. One after the other, to growing waves of laughter:

First he was seen "giving the Aussies a hand in the ashes," carrying drinks off the famous Lord's cricket turf in full whites. Next he was at the 2013 U.S. Open, peering over Andy Murray's shoulder as he hoisted the trophy. The show moved on to the 2013 NBA Championship, Bails' mouth wide in a boastful shout, arm around Lebron's shoulders as the confetti rained down. Then with Bayern Munich – Champions League winners, in the on-field team photograph with the trophy. Soon he was "going for a run in Spain," a picture showing a wide-eyed game-face on Bails running with the Bulls.

It wasn't just sporting events he had visited though. He was "Hanging with Barack at the White House," seated in the Oval Office, an earnest face of instruction as he coached a clearly engaged Obama. Next he was "gaining entry into the royal family," Bails' angry face overlaid on the new baby's as Will and Kate posed for the paps.

As the players slapped their legs and wiped tears from their eyes, the music died down, giving way to the final slide that simply read:

"Creating a No. 1, chart-topping music hit..."

The subtle bass line of the soundtrack of his pièce de résistance slowly began: the #Bails remix of Robin Thicke's "Blurred Lines."

Set to an infectious beat by musical genius Pharrell Williams, this song had become an internet sensation thanks to a film clip without much to it. A little bit of the singer, a guest appearance by a rapper, a few hashtags, and a handful of gorgeous models wearing very little.

Bails had spent a good few days with the IT guys, having them superimpose him using a greenscreen camera shot. It looked like he was dancing in the scene with Pharrell, Thicke, and the bevy of beauties.

The players erupted at the cheeky grin and ridiculously understated dance moves of Bails, larger-than-life in front of them. By the end, they were literally rolling out of their seats with laughter.

When the lights came back on, the slow clap began - a player invented ritual that was only done in-house, to show appreciation and acceptance for anyone who spoke to the group that they really vibed with. It went once, twice, three and then an unprecedented four rounds.

He was back. And the players loved him.

END ZONE
WE TALK LEGACY & LOVE

When I arrived a few minutes prior to one of Bails' scheduled radiation treatments, Caron was the only one in his room. The bathroom door was open, the light off. The bed was empty. Sipping at a steaming cup of tea and leafing through a magazine, Caron sat in a chair by the window. She looked up when I came in.

"He was meant to go in at 2:40," she said by way of greeting, waving with her cup toward the empty bed, "but they must have gotten in a bit earlier."

"How long...? What, um...? How long is he in the...?" It was difficult to settle on one question. Bails' condition was deteriorating, no matter how calm she seemed as she waited for this one treatment. "What does the radiation involve nowadays?"

"Oh, it's like ten, fifteen minutes."

"I'm picturing an x-ray machine or a CT machine." Like something we have our athletes in almost weekly for various injuries, but with much more riding on the results.

"Yeah, it's like that," she confirmed, putting her magazine on the floor beside her chair. "And you just go through the big donut, I think. So it's a bit uncomfortable, 'cos I think he's gotta lie on his stomach, which is really painful for him. So they give him an extra shot of morphine before he goes down. But yeah, it's not long at all." She glanced over at the clock. "Been a little bit longer this time." A touch of worry crept into her voice.

"So it's pretty targeted?" I hooked one of the other chairs with my foot – there were three in total – and dragged it closer to Caron.

"Yeah, it's like the rays are on that one" – she pointed to the spot on her own ribcage where the biggest lump was on Bails' side– "and they just sort of shoot down. When they set it out at the start, they get a bit of wire, and they go around the areas and they sort of go down the middle of the back..." She sketched out the path with her finger. "They must measure it out and then they know exactly what they're doing when each one gets there, I suppose."

"Is this bout having the same effect as last time?" I laid out my notebook and pens and a bottle of water on the rolling table by the bed.

"Yeah, I think so. Like he'll say, 'Have a look' and it's hard to not say, 'Oh yeah, it's working!'"

We both laugh in spite of ourselves at that bit of gallows humor, but it was true. Bails had told me he couldn't tell anymore, and maybe he didn't want to know the truth.

"Triggy brought this man in," Caron began, "David Seymour-Smith. Ten years ago he went through the same thing, nice man."

"Oh yeah. Yeah, yeah, Triggy mentioned that." He'd mentioned something about it a couple of days ago back at work. "What's the full story again?"

"Ten years ago had lung cancer," Caron began, "but not the same as Dean's. His primary was the kidney, so he had that removed, but it had made it to the lung. Now his brother-in-law had been to Vietnam, and he had bladder cancer, and he started using this treatment. It's from apricot kernels..."

She reached for the magazines on the floor and pulled a sheet of paper from one of them. "I printed this out for Dean; there are heaps on the internet. Turns out a lot of people with cancer use it as a sort of complementary medicine." After skimming it, she handed it to me.

"Something in it turns into cyanide," She continued her explanation, "and that effectively kills the cancer cells but leaves the normal cells. So, this started ten years ago, when they told him he had three months to live. So, yeah. It was good just for Dean to hear that – he said, 'Oh, bet your food tastes like this,' and they shared stories. He said it was like a flashback for him, looking at Dean. He said, *'That was me.'*"

"Oh, so he came in?" I had thought it was just someone Triggy knew of, from whom he'd gotten the story.

Caron nodded. "He came in here, yeah, with Triggy, and yeah." She wasn't sure what to describe first. "He said he was like in the seventy kilo range, he'd lost so much weight, and he looked exactly like that, saying all this stuff... I was talking 'bout him with our doctor, just to say what do you think of it. And he said, 'Yeah look, people have used it, but Dean's cancer's different.' And I said 'I understand that but he just thinks he's just lying here to die now, like there's nothing." The pain in her voice was palpable.

"Dean does or the doctor does?"

"Nah, Dean. Well yeah, both really. We have a palliative doctor now, so that says a lot."

She paused, contemplating the inevitable for just a moment. I did the same, counting off the number of signals that the end was nigh. The list seemed to be growing by the visit, keeping pace with the tumor. His request for Mitch. The failed return home. The increase in side effects from different drugs, the decrease in his mobility. The palliative care doctor. Now there was an alternative treatment. This was the last roll of the dice, I thought.

Caron almost read my mind. "So I said, 'Well, we may as well give it a crack, it's not gonna hurt 'ya. The only side effect that David had was just nausea for half an hour, and he's putting up with more than that right now. He just gets it in from Victoria, all this stuff. It's like $90 for a month. It's not expensive.

You can go to places like Mexico and I think they inject it into people, which is a lot more expensive."

"First you'd have to get there."

"Exactly! How would you get there when you're already so shit, you know? He can't even walk around the ward!"

"And did he like the idea of it or what?" I gave the paper back to her; her hands shook as she folded it up.

"Yeah," she said with a sigh and a wave of her hand, "yeah, I think. He just said today, '*What do you reckon?*' And I said 'Well, once we've talked to the doctors and as long as it's not gonna interfere with any of the other things that you're on, why not have a crack? Yeah, you just grind them up with a coffee grinder, and David just has them with some pineapple juice. He just said, '*I just try and take it down in one gulp*.' And he still takes it to this day."

She took a moment to slip the paper between the pages of a magazine once more. When she spoke again, her voice was steadier.

"He also said, 'I got all the stress out of my life.' He used to run a big corporation. They recently asked him to do something, chair some board, and he just said, 'Look, I'm flattered, but I just can't do it 'cos I know it'll bring stress to me.'"

"So has he still got...? 'Cos I know Nick Poulos, when he explained his cancer to me, that he sort of still has it– and he always will."

"Yeah, that's the thing. David said, '*You've got to come to terms with how you can live with it the best. All you're doing here is you're worrying about Caron and the boys and what their life's going to be and blah blah blah, but it's what you do.*' He said he did exactly the same thing until he thought, '*Okay, well if I'm not going to get rid of it, how can I live the best with it?*' Once he sort of became at peace with that, he just thought, well, every day's a bonus from that point.'"

"Interesting he said that, 'cos when I was last in Bails said something like, *'Every day I wake up, I'm pretty happy.'*"

With a sad laugh, Caron said, "Yeah. But he just got upset a moment before you arrived, and he said, *'I don't wanna die. I just don't wanna die.'*"

The line hung in the air, words that were always implied here but rarely spoken.

"And I'm like, 'Well, no one wants you to!'" Caron laughed. I had to laugh along with her. "Obviously that's all you think. How could you not? And you just feel like shit."

I nodded. "It must be so hard," talking directly to Caron now, "and I'm blessed that I've never had to do it. When I was in the Development role, I had to try and put myself in their shoes. Or in the parents' shoes or their girlfriend's shoes. And I've always found that pretty easy. But thinking about –"

I catch myself fudging my words, and correct the vague for the concrete.

"Well, not thinking, actually knowing that the end is so close. I just can't imagine it."

"Yeah, the end. Nup. You can't. Maybe if you were over 70," she laughs, not a happy sound, "but no."

We sat in silence for a minute. The sadness was heavy, but Caron had no more tears to cry right now. Or perhaps she was saving them, knowing there would be more spilled soon than ever before. My eyes surprised me with moisture instead, and I blinked the tears away. My lengthy one-on-one with Caron while Bails was elsewhere forced me to contemplate this new normality: my connection to Bails would soon be only through Caron, and the boys of course.

"Darcy came in this morning," Caron moved on to happier things thankfully. "I said, *'How did you go last night?'*"

"Oh yeah, how did he go?"

"Apparently, he did well. Like he would never say anything. But Mitchell says, *'Nah, I think he did really well.'*"

207

I threw out a small fist pump. I couldn't wish for enough good things for the two boys right now.

"Mitchell went to help," Caron continued her commentary on the game, "so Darcy didn't like that, knowing he'd be there. I said 'Why don't you like that, what is it?' and he said, *'Oh, I just don't want people to think that we're both here, like they've given it to us both as a handout'*. And that's natural that they're both gonna think like that a bit."

I scrunch my nose up. "You know what they say: the people who matter don't care, and those that care don't matter."

"Exactly!" Caron was emphatic. "But I said to him, 'You know what? They can go and get stuffed. Do people even know why you're getting picked? You get picked at the Crows 'cos Glenelg's not gonna pick 'ya! Do they wanna be that? Well, good for them! It's not like you're getting some big opportunity. You're getting paid less than you might elsewhere, and it's 'cos someone else has agreed that you're not good enough.' And Mitchell's got a degree, he hasn't just slipped in there.'"

"That's pretty well put!" I agreed with a little chuckle. Two of Caron's more endearing sides – that of the fierce protector and no-nonsense country girl – made her seem right in her element. I admired her strength even more now than ever, but kept it to myself. "There's no argument to that one."

"Exactly! Stevo took him aside and said, *'I know what you're hearing, people saying he's only got there because of his dad. But you've had that all your life.'* And Darcy said, *'Yeah, I have – every time I get on a side, people say that. So it doesn't bother me'*. He's pretty laid back about it; he's pretty off the cuff."

As she finished a passionate update on her son's fortunes, I marvelled at the unique strength she displayed. Not just now, but as long as I had known her, Caron at once combined a lack of pretense with grace, care and courage. She would soon need every ounce of it.

208

The door opened again, but this time the nurse did more than just pop her head inside. She pushed it all the way open and held it for Bails to come through. He moved slow, shuffling a bit, a caricature of the tired and sick. I caught a quick look of bone-deep sadness on Caron's face, only there for a second and then gone again.

"Mitch was quite up and about the first day he was in," I began, hoping to bridge that awkward moment and try to lighten the mood. "A bit chirpy."

"I think he just likes being around the boys," Caron added, "and the fitness boys too."

The first nurse hurried around to the other side of the bed as another nurse followed Bails inside. As she passed around the end of the bed, a little too close to the wall, she knocked a clipboard to the floor with a clatter. "Oh, sorry, the other one's up there. It came off... sorry."

Bails bent to pick up the clipboard. "You need that one too?" He gestured to the one that still hung on the wall. Still helping. Still treating everyone the same. Even when he was the one on death's door.

The second nurse took it from him. "Yeah. I'll take those notes there too. Thanks for picking 'em up." She and the other nurse checked over the notes on the clipboards as Bails levered himself onto the bed.

"Didn't take too long, did it?" Caron asked him. "Just the hip today, was it?"

"Yeah." He didn't elaborate, just swung his legs up onto the mattress with a bit of help from his hands. The only sound in the room came from the whiny overhead light, before his sheets added a faint rustle as he adjusted the sheets and pillow. I pushed the wheeled table a little closer so he could reach the plastic cup of water there.

"Thanks for that," Caron told the first nurse.

"No problem," she replied and followed the other nurse out the door.

"You gonna sit there?" Caron asked Bails as she gathered up her things. "Paddy can sit on the side, and I'll head off in a minute. I'll come back later, okay?"

"Yeah." There was no animation in his voice. He was noticeably quieter, drained, yellow. His skin looked almost like aged paper stretched over his bones. For the first time, he looked close to defeat.

"You want anything to eat?" Caron asked him. "Or would you like to wait?"

"You want a drink?" I asked, reaching for the water on his rolling table.

"Nah," he waved me away, "I'm right."

"See 'ya," Caron told him quietly and leaned down to kiss him. "See 'ya later, after Pilates. I'll come back. Okay?" She couldn't quite keep the worry out of her voice. Then she turned to me. "See 'ya, Paddy."

"See 'ya, Caron." I waited until she was gone, and the door had clicked shut once more, before I turned to Bails.

"How do you normally feel after the radiation?" I asked him, placing my phone as close as possible so that it picked up his fading voice. "Does it knock you around a bit? Or is that less troublesome than the chemo?"

"Radiation only goes for..." He paused to catch his breath, "a short period of time. Depends on what you have done." Another pause. His voice strained. "Fifteen minutes, twenty max. Chemo, I could be sitting there for..." He paused, trying to swallow. "If I've got two drugs, could be an hour the first one, an hour and a half the second one." He paused yet again, this time to cough. "So, radiation's a bit more intense, a shorter period of time."

"Yeah." Either way, it seemed to take a lot out of him. I poured him more water, more to give him a minute to catch his breath rather than rehydrate. After a moment, I asked my next question. "You get to see the game at all? No Fox Footy here, I can see, but the score?" Small talk first.

"Heard it on the radio. Listening to the radio, seem to be pretty..." Pause again, scratchy breath. "High handball, high stats. Happens every year with the first and second game."

"Yeah, they mucked around with it," I was blunt. "The ball was hot, slippery. Looked like we fumbled a bit too."

"Opposition was better," he agreed with a nod. "Their intensity was better."

We dissected the game in staccato bursts of clichés and analogies, and Bails seemed right at home. Analysis complete, he turned to the next game.

"Might not be a bad game, too, with GWS next." He frowned. "That's who we got? GWS in Sydney?"

"Yep, that's not for another—what, ten days? Twelve days? So still a while."

He started putting the pieces of our buildup together. "We played an undermanned Port. Carlton. Then... We'll play a good Giants team."

"Yeah, but a good Giants team isn't that good just yet," I added.

"Yeah," he agreed, "would've been better if we could play a North Melbourne or someone, a couple of good hit outs."

"Yep. 'Cos walking off that into Geelong for round one, gonna be a big slap in the face."

He paused for a drink of water and then asked, "He went off at 'em at half time?"

Surprised, I had to assume he had heard about Sando's half time "intervention" from one of the other coaches. "Yeah, he wasn't that bad actually. He didn't say anything on the field, he got down in the rooms, beat all the coaches in there, and he just got the players in the room by himself. The players said they thought he was gonna erupt, but he was quite measured. He wanted to blow up, but he just said, *'Good news is, that's the worst*

211

I've seen you play. Shithouse. If we start playing like Crows, we'll beat this team by ten goals.' So it was actually a positive message about what's coming, as opposed to what's gone. So he did it well."

"Mm. Yep, no doubt. How are the young kids?" His voice faded out at the end there; I almost couldn't hear him. I perhaps only deciphered it because I knew of his love for watching the youngsters develop.

"The ones that played?"

He made an assenting sound and waved me on, telling me to keep talking.

"I think they all... *we* were all sloppy." I made this disclaimer before discussing individuals, remembering our discussion a few visits back about coaches taking responsibility too. We talked through the youngsters, then the new free agents, then his project players, and last but not least, the leaders. He always reveled in this talk, and for a few minutes I was almost sure he was imagining himself back in his office.

The faint smell of wet socks hung in his office like a morning fog over the practice field, but we barely noticed. This was a standard aroma, as familiar to us as bread to a baker, or grease to a mechanic.

Bails was playing with the magnets on his whiteboard as we talked about the names that were written on some of them.

"So they're trying to deal with it in house." I spoke in hushed tones, even despite the closed door. The issue at hand was a small infraction – though the media would not have seen it that way – which we didn't want to cause waves, internal or external.

"The leaders need to understand, though Paddy," Bails turned to emphasize his points, "*'Leadership'* isn't punishment, or titles."

I nodded, fully agreeing with him. "If that's all it is it becomes a cliché. People throw the word around so much."

In my eyes, and it seemed Bails shared the view, it's both impossible and vital to talk about the important stuff in sport, or life without using clichés that make eyes glaze over, mouths yawn and ears shut down.

"All these leadership programs," Bails continued the thread as he grouped a few select names at the top of the board, "and the media - they've reduced the word to such a throwaway that it's getting hard to tell what a '*leader*' really is."

His first grouping of names on the board had a clear theme, which became clear as he elaborated.

"The thing is, even though it can be a cliché, you know when you come across a *real* leader 'cos they're not a cliché at all."

He could easily have been talking about himself here. Bails was the opposite of typical, a unique character.

"You're right," I nodded. "A real leader can get you to do certain things that deep down you think are good and want to be able to do, but usually can't get yourself to do on your own."

I thought of my own examples – a great teacher in high school; an extremely cool older player I had wanted to emulate; and the understated coach standing just in front of me.

"They could have the title," Bails continued, "but you don't follow because of that, or their name, or because of some punishment. You love what they stand for – you love them – so you wanna follow."

He had always challenged me with ideas, making sure I was doing what was right rather than what everyone else did. This was no exception, and I loved it.

"If we can help unleash a couple of them in our group," Bails ended his monologue, "that's magic."

Perhaps by design, but more likely because he was a perfect example of this exact type of leader, I was inspired by the time I left his office.

Unfortunately, more pressing issues than our thoughts on the leaders bought him back to the room.

"What's that oxygen on, mate?" he rasped, nodding toward the oxygen tap in the wall next to his bed, the source that feeds his nose tubes.

I got up and took a couple of steps closer so I could see the readout. "It's between two and three?" I didn't know if that was good or bad.

"Yeah, that's right." Shifting again, he closed his eyes.

"What else, what else...?" He tapped his fingers on the mattress.

"Um..." I really couldn't think of a thing just then.

"How's your position?" he asked me, interested in my development as much as the players.

"On the bench? Yeah, super busy the last couple of weeks, 'cos we've got so many rotations with six on the bench. But otherwise it's not too bad. I don't see much of the game."

"That's what Doc said last year. He was everywhere but the game."

"Yeah. I can see why – to be able to coach anyone, to be able to give them feedback on what you're seeing. It's hard. I'm gonna try and make it a bit of a positive, in that it'll force the players to start to identify their own problems. Gotta start leading themselves."

There was a knock on the door and a nurse walked in. "Hi," she said to both of us and then turned to Bails, all business. "You haven't had your dexamethasone."

"Oh really?" Bails looked puzzled.

"So I'll just get you that."

"What did I have before I went down to radiation?" he asked. "Pat gave me something– I don't know what it was."

214

"Um, who gave it to 'ya?" It was her turn to look puzzled.

"Um, Pat I think it was."

"No, I'm Pat. I didn't give it to you."

Bails' confusion was understandable at this point; I had already seen three different nurses just in this visit. Add in his treatment fatigue, and the fact he had been here for weeks now, and a little forgetfulness was understandable.

"Who's the other lady who works this room?"

"Toni."

"Toni," he repeated. "Toni gave me a pill, sorry."

"Did she? I'll just check." As quickly as she'd breezed in, she breezed out again.

"Extra cover for the radiation, yeah?" I observed.

"I dunno. I take so many pills." He shook his head. "Who were we talking about?"

"Um, the bench? There was a lot more talk this week though..."

Pat returned before we could get into it again, knocking on the door even as she opened it. "She did, but she didn't give you the Dex, okay, so I'll give you that now."

"Thanks," Bails told her.

She walked over to Bails' bedside table and set down a small plastic cup, then picked up the bottle to refill with water at the sink.

"How long were you waiting for?" Bails asked me. "Wouldn't have been too long, would it?"

"Nah," I shook my head, "only here for ten minutes, talking to Caron. Broke a few speeding limits before I got here."

"Yeah, wasn't too long, only did my hip today."

"How do they decide what they do and what they don't do?"

"Dunno, actually."

"I've just gotta watch you take that," Pat told Bails, pushing the little cup to where he could reach it, "and then I'll do a set of obs. Thanks, Dean."

"Yep." he said, picking up the cup and tossing back the contents before turning to me. "What's the newspaper say today?"

Nurse Pat moved to the side of the bed to begin her obs. "Do you want me to move?" I asked her, feeling a bit in the way.

She waved a hand at me. "No, no, I'll be fine. I'm used to maneuvering around people. I've got eight grandkids... not quite as big as you, though!" She smiled as she said that, kind of in impish glint in her eye, and I had to laugh. It got a snort of laughter from Bails, too.

"Just put that on your finger, love," she told Bails, handing him something small.

"I like your name, Patricia," I told the nurse with a smile. "My name's Patrick."

She paused in what she was doing and glanced over at me with a big grin. "Ah, your pulse is a bit better," Pat turned back to her duties, "ninety-six now instead of a hundred and two. All right, I have to ask you that question – whether you've been to the bathroom or not today?"

"Nah, not today," he said. "Yesterday I've been."

Another glance at me, then, "No privacy here, is there, Dean?"

"No."

We watched in silence as Pat packed up her equipment onto a wheeled cart that she pulled in from the hall. Bails rasped a quick "Thank you" again as she pushed it through the door.

"You wanna move at all?" I asked Bails once she was gone.

"Nah, I'm okay." He glanced sideways, first at me where I was shifting my things on the floor and then standing up.

"Okay. You get the email I flicked through?" I dropped back down into my usual chair.

"On?" he started, but then remembered. "Oh, the questions and that? Yeah." He gazed down at something on his bed. I glanced and saw his phone, with a new message on it. "My parents are about to walk in, in fifteen minutes."

I nodded. "Okay, should I pick one of the questions and ask you? Or do you wanna leave it till another time?" If he wanted to be alone with his parents, that took priority at this stage.

"Nah, just pick one and I'll see if I can answer it."

"All right..." As I thumbed through the list of questions on my phone, he shifted his position. His skinny, bare legs were exposed on the bed now, highlighting how frail he had become. "Let's go with one that's a bit general. When you look back over your time in football, what's the common theme that stands out or comes up for you?"

"What's the common theme that comes out? Between football and life?"

"Yeah."

Hands gripping the edge of the mattress, he swung his feet as he thought about what to tell me. I let him take his time on it, not interrupting his thought process, ready to receive whatever he could dispense.

"I think there's a little bit of... expect the unexpected, you know?" His answer was unexpected. The wet cough that followed wasn't.

"You're always challenged with different things each day," he picked up where he left off. "Different situations, players, personnel, you know. Every day there's a little twist that you gotta be wary of, not looking for, but just be open. There's a few things that happen, just some unexpected stuff, nothing that's too dramatic. But sometimes things will fall your way, too, that you don't expect."

He stopped to lean over and take a sip of water.

"You know, I had players at Melbourne, as an example, one player turned up to training not in a great way. He was about to do a press conference on a Monday morning, but he was still intoxicated. You don't expect that."

217

"You sure don't!" I agreed, although I had seen it before too.

"The players' abilities to handle the pressure from outside, the public pressure. Sometimes even the teammates' pressure. It's all about handling the unexpected, the unknown, the future. That's the challenge."

About halfway through his answer, a burst of activity started just outside the room. Equipment rattled as it rolled past, voices rose and faded. I got up and closed the door.

"What was the best way you found to handle that stuff?" I asked, returning to my chair. "When shit came up that you were just not ready for?"

"Oh," he pondered for a second, "just try and come to a resolution as quickly as you can. Try and come up with a plan until you, or the player, are back in control. And then have faith that it will work out okay. It usually does."

I nodded. So simple, but so profound given where he sat right now.

"See every day is just a different day," he pressed on. "You know what 80 percent of the day is gonna be, but 20 percent of it could throw up a massive curveball. Or it could be nothing. You've just gotta work to stay ahead, and stay on your toes. If you let things linger - which can happen, 'cos no one solves all the problems..." Bails coughs again, this one as heavy as I'd heard yet. He picks up where he left off once he spits out the product of his coughing. "If you let a few things linger, then they become distractions, and before you know it, you're in a meeting about it when it could've been fixed ages ago."

I laughed at that. Good to see his hatred for beating around the bush was still as strong as ever.

I wanted to make sure we didn't miss anything. "Anything else?"

"Well there is one more thing," Bails nodded. "Particularly in a team sport, the team will continue to exist when you're gone, life will go on. The reason you were able to do that wasn't just 'cos of you and your amazing talents. It was because there were others around you. And that's what it should be about when it finishes. What you leave behind. Your legacy."

With zero effort, he struck such a chord that it almost knocked the breath out of me. I paused for a moment to let the weight of the statement sink in. A cough from Bails reminded me that time wasn't something we had much of, so I moved ahead.

"And across your – all the different team environments you've been in, and this includes the amateur stuff as well – Mount Gravatt – what's the common theme? Strip away the superstars and the level that it's at, and the difference between a red and a yellow sash..."

"Um," he pondered again, then took a deep breath to answer. "Ah, there's still that feeling, that tribal feel amongst players, that group power. You know, once you become part of a group, it's a very strong thing to be in. That's still the same, whether it's at Mount Gravatt, Essendon, or Adelaide. People love to be in a strong group. And when they feel they can achieve within a group, they get good support, they get, um, guidance, then they... they tend to succeed."

"When the group supports itself a little bit?"

"Yeah, the group not only supports itself, but pushes itself and challenges itself, in a good way. Then you get out of the group what they want to achieve, and then you ask: can this group actually achieve that or is it just too far away?"

He grew more animated as he spoke, and his thoughts drifted back from the past to the boys who had been in his charge.

"I think we could be in a Grand Final or we could win in the next three years," he said with certainty. Thinking for a moment, he decided he needed to add more detail. "It might not be this year, it might not be next year, it might not, might, might, might. But the thing is our age group, and our list, we might not be that far away." Another cough, and another sip of water.

I wanted to keep him rolling, but his own passion did that for me.

"But the players drive it," he kept on. "The players drive it, and other players jump on board. The more players drive it, the more players jump on board. Then all of a sudden you've got fifteen to twenty players who are driving it, and you got another ten who are jumping on board 'cos they know they can be a part of something strong. And they love it."

"Weight of numbers," I slapped a label on it for him. "Have you worked with a group who's harnessed that and played even better or even achieve above what they should?"

"Um," he considered for a longer time than normal here. His answer was clear when he gave it. "I think the Bombers weren't a great example... woulda' been nice for them to win another premiership. Port Adelaide certainly shoulda' won another one. I think the first year here with Adelaide is the one where you can say, if you like, we overachieved in a sense. I think we thought we were going okay, but I think external expectations weren't close to where we finished. You know what I mean."

I did. What we achieved in that first year, going from 14th to one score away from a Grand Final, was one of the most rewarding experiences of my career.

"See," Bails continued, "I think with this group, you can stretch this group to the next level. I think that's a good thing. I think that's a good sign. Particularly when you're facing adversity, that's a nice strength to have – a group of blokes who are prepared to stretch beyond."

That was an interesting addition to the conversation that I hadn't prompted him on: adversity. I picked it up and ran with it.

"So you're saying that group culture," I probed for more, "is more powerful when there's adversity rather than when they're going well?"

"I think that when you look at..." a pause as another cough, sudden and hard, tore from his throat. Like an exhausted runner on the final stretch, he gathered himself and pressed on.

"If you look at a team who's sort of exceeded a bit of their own expectation, I think that's really important to have those guys who are prepared to stretch themselves for each other, and achieve a little bit more than what people might think that they can."

Yet again, he had mentioned doing things for others, and he had even used the word *love* more than once in the past few minutes. Was that really what was behind the sort of selflessness Bails exemplified?

The buzzing, humming, clicking, beeping silence fell once more as I tried to digest all he'd said while Bails laid back on the bed and closed his eyes, exhausted. His phone trilled, but he didn't move to answer it, and it finally stopped. I thought perhaps he'd fallen asleep until he turned his head to look out the window at a bird that had landed on the sill outside.

"That your phone ringing before?" I asked.

"Mm, probably," he answered, still watching the bird.

I reached for his phone and tapped the message icon. "Missed call from Chappy. Was just checking if it might be your folks coming up. They know your room, don't they?"

"Who's that?" He frowned, mental fatigue kicking in.

"Your folks."

"Oh, yeah, yeah," he waved, "don't worry, Mum'll just walk in!"

I laughed and then tried to gather my thoughts. A return to one of his favourite books beckoned.

"In the last chapter of that *Power of Habit* book, they were talking about the fact you can go through all these steps to change habits or make that shift. But there's always that higher purpose, meaning, something else. Like, Alcoholics Anonymous have Jesus, the Colts had Tony Dungy's son, they all have something that unifies and feels like something bigger."

"Yeah," Bails nodded along. "Yeah, for us it's the love of the club. You walk in, and you're a lot stronger when you walk through the door than when you walk out of it. 'Cos you're surrounded by your teammates, if you like, but when you walk out you're a little bit on your own. No, I'd agree with that. I reckon that's a pretty powerful thing to have." His voice trailed off, and I mentally noted another mention of love.

"Do you want me to give you a few minutes before your folks get here?" I asked. "Let you catch your breath?"

"Yeah, they'll be here in a minute."

As I got up, he reached out and grabbed my arm. "Tell me more about the footy, Paddy, I wanna know what's happening."

I was happy to oblige—it didn't feel like time to leave yet. I sat back down and we talked what he loved again. It was me doing most of the talking this time, answering the questions he asked: How did we go on the weekend? Who's up and who's not? Can Coach X be a senior coach? Can Coach Y win a flag with his style? And why would anyone be a coach in the first place?

As I waited for his answer on the last question, he began to cough, violently. My gaze wandered about the room, falling on the paper cup toward the center of the table. The conversation was so compelling I'd forgotten that I'd bought him a hot chocolate as a bit of a treat.

"Damn, I forgot your hot chocolate," I pushed the cup toward him until it was within his reach. "Been sitting over here for a while. It's just chocolate now, not hot at all!"

He took a moment to study the cup, and then cleared his throat. He took a slow breath.

"I guess coaching is a little like this cup," he said, holding the cup up in his weak grasp. "The purpose of a cup isn't to hold

222

onto what it has – it's to pass it on, and pour it into something else. My mouth, in this case, but it could be another cup."

Still dry, even when dishing out wisdom.

"That's why you coach," he added a personal touch to finish, making the analogy his own. "It's why you mentor. It's not about you; it's about passing on what you have inside you, to fill someone else up."

Stuck for words, I just nodded. I almost welled up in tears: not only was his simple example so good, it was exactly what he had been doing for me. Every visit, he had filled me up with more than I had before I walked in. I felt so full right now that my chest almost burst.

As he slipped into one of his micro-sleeps, I wiped the tears from my eyes and made a note that perhaps summed him up the best:

Pour what you have into something bigger than you.

"Okay, mate." Back in the room after his 20-second timeout, Bails called time for today. He hadn't noticed how profound I found his analogy to be.

"Bails, mate," I tried an unplanned attempt at gratitude on the buzzer, limited as much by the lump in my throat as I was by time. "Thank you so much. For everything."

Coughs meant he couldn't answer, but he waved what I interpreted as a "don't mention it." Familiar voices grew closer outside the door – to me they sounded like Bev and Ted.

"Hang in there," I told him as I gathered up my things and headed for the door. "We'll chat more next time."

I had no idea how wrong I was.

HUDDLE

TAPERING

Over the next week, things deteriorated quickly for Bails. His one-line response to a "How 'ya goin'" text a couple of days later was a small hint:

No, Paddy feeling tired mate.

I could see signs of the inevitable growing closer when he cancelled a visit on the other side of the weekend.

Paddy I am full up today and tired. My
parents are also spending time with me.

A similar response the next week, when trying to get a visit in before flying to Sydney for a pre-season game against the Giants, really had my alarm bells ringing.

The week has been rough, Paddy. I am no
good in the mornings, so before 9 I can't do.

Finally, we locked something in.

Saturday arvo should be ok.

Come Saturday, I wanted to check before the long drive down South.

Still ok for a visit this arvo Bails? I am
thinking around 2:30ish.

Yes 30 min should be ok.

Partially out of habit, and part ceremony, I stopped off to grab a pizza roll and a hot chocolate. I didn't need a coffee, as I had already had four in various meetings with players on the way back from Sydney. And I knew he wouldn't be able to eat the roll, or drink the beverage. But a part of me wanted to maintain the pattern, thinking that would stave off the impending change that was gaining momentum.

All the coffee in the world couldn't come close to the jolt from what I saw as I entered the room.

It had been ten days since I sat with Bails when he was finally feeling up for another chat. The guy I visited last time, although tired and sorry-looking, had since left the room. In his place was a sick stereotype, like a character from a zombie movie. Yellow, drawn, shrunken, with all of his extremities in constant state of flexion, not able to straighten his legs or arms or fingers.

Not that he would've known this though. With his eyes half rolled back in his head, Bails was elsewhere. From the pantomime that was the intermittent movement of his arms, his body suggested that, in his mind at least, Bails had stepped back out onto the training track. Reaching to move cones, pointing further afield, turning his head to see what the defenders were doing behind the ball.

Knowing that time was short, his parents had come in to be close. Bev sat dutifully at the foot of the bed, still massaging his feet even as he twitched. Positive as always, she welcomed me to the room with a big smile. Ted was more subdued in the corner. He said "Hi" but didn't take the dialogue much further, as he composed himself. The water pooled on the bottom eyelid of each eye suggested he had been elsewhere too. Perhaps harking back to a time when his young boy was unstoppable. Perhaps thinking ahead to the horrible reality that was now so close: soon his boy would no longer be in his life.

They filled me in on how he could hear but would "take rests" like this. Fifteen minutes was about the longest he could stay in the room today, but he'd be back soon, no doubt. In an attempt to coax him back earlier, Bev pointed out to him – in a louder voice, as if he was just deaf instead of on death's door – that I was in the room.

Bails' eyes focused for a moment, and he lifted his head an inch or two. He tried to talk, but all that came was a wheezy breath. He dropped his head back to the pillow and resumed his pantomime.

Unnerved, but appreciating that my emotions were nothing compared to what his parents may be experiencing in seeing this, I sat in the chair that I'd become so familiar with, and asked them how they were faring.

Positive as always, they compared what they were feeling to Dean, and said they just had to keep helping. The silence that followed said more than they had cared to elaborate; they both knew they wouldn't need to keep that brave face up much longer.

VOICE

I placed the laptop I had carried in on the table, trying not to disturb the space the parents had created with their son. It was Bev who broke the silence and moved things forward.

"Dean," she spoke loud and slow, one hand on his leg and the other pointing to the MacBook I was opening, "Paddy's got something to show you."

In the lead up to the season, as culmination of the conversations we had with the leaders around what they wanted to stand for as a group, the final piece was a short video. Five minutes long, it expanded on the journey the group had been through so far since we all arrived, but also focused on what was still to come, and why it meant so much to everyone.

"I wanted to ask you a couple of things about this little project– you know we've done this before, getting right down into the players' hearts – that first Crows video we did when we arrived. It's like that but looks more at some of the stuff we've spoken about. The tribe."

Bails grunted as he sat up, Bev and I both helping to lift his bony shoulders.

"Well, we've done that again, and it's pretty sweet, but I wanted to take some of the stuff we've recorded from our chats in here and overlay it on the video. Would you be okay with that?"

"Yeah," Almost a word - more a breath - but a slight nod of the head to accompany it helped me decipher his answer.

I played the video: interviews with players - the young men he had helped grow up - talking about what the team meant to them. Overlays of inspirational plays, tackles and other things that Bails would recognise as "Playing like a Crow," a tagline he'd thrown out in the early days, taking a leaf out of Rex Ryan's "Let's play like Jets" catch cry from the *Hard Knocks* series he loved. And as the clip came towards the end with the background music in lull, a black screen appeared.

"Where's my voice?" He asked, confused.

"It isn't on it yet," I replied as his words flashed up on the screen in silence. "I wanted to check with you to make sure it was ok."

His response was faint, but crystal clear. "I want them to hear my voice."

I put a hand on his shoulder and squeezed a physical reassurance, nodding to let him know I would make sure they heard him. His bony shoulder carried almost no muscle now, and it jolted with another coughing fit as I held onto him.

As the coughing subsided, and Bev moved to help him with tissues, I thought it best to leave him with his parents. I close the Mac, watching the last of his words from the video that were frozen on the screen:

It's important to have those guys who are willing to stretch themselves, and achieve a little bit more than what people might think they can.

It spoke so much of the guy who had spoken the words. A working-class footballer who had made the big league as a player, and then made it to the top of the game as a coach too. He achieved more than anyone would've ever imagined the boy in his parents' backyard might have.

As I began to pack up my stuff, he looked up, with an unusually clear and steady gaze, and held out his hand to shake mine – something he hadn't done for a while.

And when I took his hand to shake it, the grip was strong. Firm. Almost like a vice. Nothing like the wet fish he normally gives.

He looked me dead in the eye. 'I'll see you next time," he rasped.

I fumbled a response, overcome by what this actually was. It wasn't just "see 'ya soon."

This was goodbye.

And he and I both knew it.

Outside, as I entered the sunlight and the cruel normality of the world continuing as if nothing was changing, the first tears came with a rush. The feeling of loss was like a gut-wrenching, chest-tightening hug from the humid air, forcing the breath from my healthy lungs in a sob, and another, and another.

At the same time, there was a hint of joy for what I had witnessed in my time with Bails. To watch someone die, and still give of his time to share his knowledge in the hope he could still help when he was gone, was more eye-opening and touching than I could have ever imagined.

Despite my eyes blurred with tears, I was finally clear again. I wanted to be like this man – like the teachers who'd taught me the same things before, but who I'd forgotten.

I went home, plugged in my phone, and started typing, while I could still hear his voice.

END

The few days after I saw Bails for the last time are a series of staccato scenes, each so vivid, yet seemingly disconnected from the normal flow of time.

It was a text from the Rev the very next day that confirmed what I already knew in my gut: we were into extra time.

> Hey Paddy: can you give me a call. Just
> had an update from Caron- not great. I'm
> going in early this arvo. MP

Given it was a Sunday afternoon, and I'd been in only yesterday, this was unusual enough.

I called, and the chat was sombre – he was deteriorating fast, so no more visitors. I know, I replied, and re-lived yesterday's visit with a lump in my throat. We talked about how things might roll out from here on, and left him to his visit.

Not long after, another text from Mark.

> Hi Paddy; give me a call when you can.
> Just stepped out of the hospital. MP.

We spoke again, and this time there was less vagary: he would leave us in the next twenty-four to forty-eight hours, no doubt. Prepare those who need to be prepped.

I called Triggy, the CEO, to give him a heads up as Captain of the ship. I called Emma, as head of Welfare, to give her a chance to clear her schedule. I told them both we would chat more tomorrow. Triggy insisted on getting one last visit; I told him to talk to Caron; it was not up to me any more, and perhaps even out of Caron's hands now.

I knew I hadn't gotten everything I wanted from him. But had he passed on everything he had wanted? Was he happy? Questions, questions, questions....

I slept, but barely.

Early Monday morning, the working group who had planned for this impending tragedy over the last month – Steven Trigg, David Noble, Emma Bahr and myself – met in the club's boardroom.

We paused the schedule halfway through that day to tell the team: no more visitors. Bails was in a bad way, and the family was battening down the hatches until further notice. As soon as we know anything, we'll let you know.

Coaches asked about when they could visit. They couldn't. Players asked if they could call. They couldn't. A couple of those closest asked if Caron still wanted the meals to continue. They could, as long as Caron knew they were coming.

The rest of the day seemed slow and yet a blur at the same time. Nothing groundbreaking would happen; we operated in a fog. I walked past Bails' office, empty but still with his hat and whistle waiting as if he was at an interstate scouting trip.

By the end of the day, I was exhausted.

I slept, deeply.

231

I woke early on Tuesday – before my normal 6am start time – thanks to the buzz on my phone. Bleary eyed, I picked it up and saw Rev's name. As if in a dream, the next thing I know I was sitting on the edge of the bed, calling him.

As it rang, I re-read the message one more time just to check I hadn't misread it:

> Hi Paddy; can you contact me ASAP. Have some news. Re: Bails. Been chatting with Caron. MP

Mark answered, and in a tired, suitably quiet voice, he broke the news.

"Hi Paddy. Unfortunately overnight, Bails passed away in his sleep. He's gone."

I stared and didn't say anything at first. Knowing it was coming, it was no shock, but my gut still felt like I'd taken a knee to the breadbasket.

"About 2 or 3 this morning," Rev continued in his measured tone, "Caron was in the room – sleeping on the floor just beside his bed. When she checked, he was gone."

I asked a few questions: How was Caron? How were the boys? Who did we need to let know? I thanked him and said I'd be in touch to talk about how we pass the news to the players and the coaches as a group.

I hung up. For a moment, the silence of the world outside in the hours before dawn made it feel like time had stopped.

My face began to contort.

I breathed in, and my chest began to ache.

I let it out, and my whole body grieved for the loss of a mentor, teacher, and friend.

Bails slept. Forever.

Everyone has times they can look back on in life, in the rear view mirror, and point to as turning points. There might be a stretch when things changed a little, or when things underwent a gradual shift, and there was a minor adjustment to be made.

Then there are events that are so stark, it is like day is all of a sudden became night. When the momentum that was inevitable tipped things into a new realm, and life would never be the same again. The moment that you knew things were out of your control, and there was nothing you could do about the big changes that were on the way. Sometimes they are obvious. Sometimes they are subtle at first, but grow over time.

I suspect the day Dean was diagnosed was like that for Caron. The first day they visited their dad in hospital was like that for Mitch and Darc. The day they said goodbye to their son for the last time was like that for Bev and Ted.

This was one of those moments for me, although that barely crossed my mind at the time – we had business to attend to. The working group got together early that day, with the sun barely coming up. We agreed to get the football department together ASAP so that they didn't find out on the radio or from a friend. The first text was to Sando.

> Hey mate, can you give me a call soon as you see this? Have some news re: Bails

With that in place, I started sending the worst text I've ever sent, sixty times over, to each player and coach:

> Hey mate, sorry for the early text but following on from the update re: bails, yesterday there's been further developments overnight. Can you please be in at the club for a 9:30 meeting in the theatre so we can speak to you guys first?
> Thanks

233

Training was cancelled, we decided, and the boys could be together to deal with it however they wanted. We had a main session the next day, and the first game of the season only nine days away. The show must go on, as Bails would say.

As the whole team gathered in the theatre, I tried to avoid eye contact. The more socially aware forced my hand – Truck caught my eye and mouthed "Bails?" with his eyebrows up. I nodded once, with closed eyes. Tex was not long after him, and just looked at me with doe-eyed shock.

"Guys, we've got an update, and it's not good." I took a breath and kept the tears at bay; I had a job to do here.

"Overnight, Bails passed away. Training today is cancelled, but we just wanted to go over a few things with you first and then you can go about your day. Rev is here, then Em, then Sando, and Triggy, then we are done."

I handed it to Mark, who spoke in more detail about how Bails passed away in his sleep, and covered some key points about what the players and staff may feel in this time of grief. Emma went over the support services offered by the AFL Players Association and the club.

Sando didn't want to speak, maintaining a brave face in front of the boys. He was as shattered as anyone in the room, and was still getting his head around the curveball his team had been thrown. Triggy said a statement would released soon, and there was no need for them to speak to anyone if they didn't want to.

With no more words to fill the void, we wrapped it up. The silence was only broken by the flapping of the theatre chairs as players began to stand. They filed out in a solemn parade, in various stages of either disbelief or grief.

Some of the players kept to themselves while others took to Twitter to express their love for the man we all knew as Bails. The same pattern played out across the entire industry. Some mentioned football: legendary coach Kevin Sheedy - the Vince Lombardi of Australian football - was one of the first to offer his respects: "Dean Bailey, a great football person with a dry wit and a sharp mind. He will be sadly missed, and our thoughts are with his family."

Most, though, shared snippets of the relationship with the man behind the football facade. Sheedy was quick to talk about the "good bloke" he knew, and the fun they had. Bernie Vince, the special project Bails had connected with in a way no coach had before, recalled their dinners: "Sad sad day!! Dean Bailey is one of the great men. So glad to have known him! Will miss our dinner dates down at Brighton! RIP mate!!"

Melbourne players, some still there, some moved on, spoke of the father figure they had lost in Bails. "He's probably one of the kindest humans I have ever come across," Captain Jack Trengove said in the press conference at their training base that morning. "He was a real father figure and role model." Brent Moloney echoed those thoughts on Twitter: "He became a real father figure to me, and we will miss him dearly. R.I.P Bails."

Port Adelaide veteran Kane Cornes had described Bails as a huge part of their historic 2004 premiership. "The best thing about footy is the people you get to meet and spend time with and he was one of those people I stayed in contact with. He was a really great footy person, really smart and had one of the best sense of humour you are ever likely to come across."

Former Power player Troy Chaplin also spoke of the tremendous person he was lucky to have as a coach: "Absolutely devastated to hear of the passing of Dean Bailey. Condolences to Caron and the kids. Such a great coach and person to know."

Even those who were coached by him in his early days at Essendon offered tribute. Ted Richards, now veteran defender and multiple premiership player at Sydney, tweeted about the start of that huge career: "Thoughts are with the Bailey family right now. Learned so much from Dean Bailey as the development coach in my first few years at Essendon."

And in the media - that constant, antagonising opponent with which he had wrestled - the reflection of the bigger picture was just as profound.

The public memorial service, a day after a private service was held close to their Brighton home, was a fitting celebration of a positive coach who had touched so many lives. Stories were shared that touched on his sense of humour, his love for the game, and his passion for helping other people be better than he was.

As the players and coaches lined the aisle for Caron, Mitch, and Darcy to walk out together, with Bev, Ted, Todd and family close behind, many saw this as the end. It marked the end of Dean as a public figure, the end of him being the topic of bar room conversations, TV panels, radio shows, and paper columns. He was now a historical figure.

It marked the end of Dean's position in the mind of worried and sympathetic supporters. For them, he was now at peace.

But for those who were close with him, he will live on in their memories, their habits, their words—some shared in publicly with a chuckle, others privately, perhaps over a coffee.

| | | |

Phil Walsh, a coach at the highest level for more than twenty years, stepped to the podium and unfolded papers as he prepared to deliver one of the toughest talks of his life. Walshy and Bails had known each other for a long time, coaching together, travelling together, and dining together with their wives, becoming as close to being family as two strangers can.

Walshy was with cross-town rival Port Adelaide, but for today at least, team colours were simply a sign of connection that was bigger than petty rivalries. Players and staff attended from more than just the Crows because for them this was personal.

He took a breath and began to eulogise the man whom thousands of people were mourning in the week before the 2014 AFL season started. He recalled their first meeting, playing against each other at Essendon's old stomping ground, Windy Hill, as young footballers in the 80's.

He described their developing relationship at Port Adelaide, where they coached together before he moved to Melbourne—a relationship that would last beyond their professional boundaries and grow even stronger over the next thirteen years.

Then, after touching on how the loss hit him, he transitioned into another gear: the coach as a motivator, without any bluster or brimstone, channelling Bails and paying him homage all at once.

"If you look up the word coach," Walshy began, "it literally means 'a vehicle that takes people from where they are to where they need to be.' No one did that better than Dean Bailey. He was a master coach.

"Some of us use fear and force to get players where they need to be. Dean Bailey quietly guided players to places they never imagined they

could get. He saw things in all of us that we didn't see in ourselves. He made us better. He cared."

The words hit home, and the tears came for the coaches and players in the room. Walshy pressed on to memories of road trips together, and when it all came together for the premiership they shared.

"Unlike so many of us in football who look for the faults and the flaws, Dean saw the positives and the potential. He had a vision for all of us, and that was to be the best we possibly could be. He'd want us all to chase our breathless moments and, like Dean did, he'd want us to do it with humility and humour. And to always remember to share our victories with those close to us.

"I loved you Bails. I'm gonna miss you so much."

"Rest in peace."

No one could've said it better.

REVIEW

This isn't the end of Bails' story.

He lives on in every habit he has taught. He lives on in every memory he has left. Evidence of his work lives on in every synapse he has remodeled, in every mind he has touched, in every person he has poured himself into. His ingenuity, his kindness, his competitiveness, his humour.

When Bernie Vince throws a tennis ball against the wall.

When David Mackay drives a different route to work.

When Rory Sloane builds a group into a community.

When Taylor Walker relaxes a tense group.

When Brenton Sanderson inspires a young footballer to believe in themselves.

When Brad Green teaches a young man how to think about defeat so that he wins next time.

When his sons become great men because they live up to his example.

What did my time with Bails do to me? It changed my life.

Reflecting on the time I had worked with him, I saw that a lot of what I thought I had discovered or built on my own was in large part due to his gentle prodding, questions and encouragement. His influence was subtle at the time, barely perceptible when looked at as isolated incidents. But looking back, his impact over a longer period is so obvious when taken as a whole.

More to the point, Bails helped me see that what I thought was important, was actually secondary – what is really important is the result of the people side of life, the result of giving yourself to a cause or a community beyond just yourself.

So with two years to go on a three-year contract at the Crows, I came to an agreement with the club and left. I stopped chasing the limelight. I stopped trying to get external recognition to tell me I was worthy, to prove how smart or hard working I was. On a personal note, I stopped trying to keep even with everyone, playing to get ahead. I stopped selfish pursuits, stopped giving time to selfish causes.

Stopping these things was only the half of it – it's what I've started that is truly a nod to Bails. I moved overseas, to the U.S.A, to study with some of the world's best in a passion I shared with Bails – the crossover of performance psychology and wellbeing. I've written the final pages of this book from a table at a window looking out on a cold city on the East Coast of the U.S., in between working as a consultant with coaches and teams over here in the NFL, NBA and MLB. I'm passing on what Bails taught me, and what I've learned since, to help improve not only the performance of the athletes and coaches, but their lives too.

Why did all this change?

Bails, a guy who had arguably gone further than anyone might've guessed early on in life, showed me a different way to look at the world:

Performance starts with people: Bails showed me that things don't have to be perfect, or look good, all the time. He exemplified the best way to grow, in any weather: to persistently do the right thing, with what you have, in whatever spot you find yourself in. That will give you the best chance to succeed at the next challenge.

There's no magic pill: He made it clear that the purpose of life isn't to stand out. Bails lived with a passion for passing on what he had, and leaving a legacy, until his last breath. By sharing with me, he showed exactly what he saw as the purpose of life: to give to your community, to change lives, not just careers.

Pour yourself into something bigger: In talking with Bails, and hearing his story, I recognized the true mark of a leader – he made everyone underneath and beside him feel better, work harder, pull together, and dig deeper. His example has inspired me to do the same, and not wait, knowing full well that the game clock is ticking for all of us.

It also inspired in me a deeper respect and admiration for the teachers I'd had along the way who were more than teachers. All of them, like Bails, had taught me more about myself than perhaps they did about the subject matter they were supposed to lead me in.

Everyone has these special teachers in their life. Maybe this makes you remember yours and re-connect with them, either in real life, virtually, or even in your memory.

Because the lessons they taught you haven't changed. They still apply. You just need to go back to them. And you can, anytime – in real life, with a phone call or a message—or in your mind, just by remembering them.

The great thing about spending time with Bails in the midst of his final battle is that he opened my eyes to what I had forgotten was important. Hopefully by sharing some of it, it may open yours while you're still in the game.

We get to keep playing. But now you know the clock is ticking.

Play on.

ACKNOWLEDGEMENTS

I'd like to thank so many people for bringing this all together, because I know now more than ever that this is a team game. The majority of this I've written based on conversations with Bails himself, keeping true to his words and the timeline of our chats, but for colour and context there are some gaps that others have filled.

First, to Caron, I owe you the deepest debt of gratitude. Not only for encouraging the idea early on, but also supporting it even after Dean had passed. Hearing the memories you shared with me was a privilege, and your love for Dean was so obvious. I hope this comes close to doing it justice. To Mitch and Darcy, your humour and strength throughout all this was amazing. At times that was enough to inspire me to keep writing when it got tough. And thanks also to the rest of Dean's family for their contributions to the story either in person or through anecdotes Bails passed on.

To Brad Green, Rory Sloane, David Mackay, Bernie Vince and Taylor Walker, for their inside stories on the coach at the coalface - I hope this lives up to your memories.

Also a big thanks to the professionals – the authors and writers – that I've been blessed to meet, who gave me some much needed feedback on my amateurish writing as I learned on the job.

To the researchers, coaches and teachers I've been fortunate enough to learn from along the way. Your wisdom infused and inspired a lot of these conversations with Bails, and he loved your work. I hope this helps others fall in love with it too.

And last but not least, my eternal thanks to Bails, for wanting to do this last challenge together. True to form, you gave everything, right to the end. On behalf of everyone you ever gave to: Thanks mate.

FORWARD PASS

I wrote this for Bails, and at the same time I wrote this for all of you.

You may have been closer to Bails than anyone. Or perhaps closer than most, but still not as close as some. You might have only known him from afar, or you may not have known him at all. The thing is, even if you didn't know him at all, I guarantee you know someone like him, and that this story has touched you in some way.

For those of you who like your coffee concentrated, I've tried to distill Bails' message – as told to me from the bed he died in – down to it's core elements. No doubt you've heard some of these before, perhaps from Bails, or maybe from another mentor. Either way, this can be a handy playbook to refer to whenever you need some guidance in your own battles as a coach, teacher, manager, parent or performer.

The one thing I ask is that you follow Bails' example and pass on whatever it gives you. You might reach back out to an old teacher or a coach. You could change the way you lead in your work or the way you relate to people at home.

Or you could simply recommend this book to someone you think will love with Bails' message, like so many other people did. In just this small way, you can play a part in helping Bails live on, by pouring his wisdom into one more person.

Cheers.